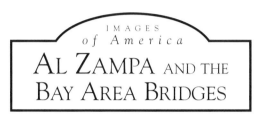

IMAGES
of America

AL ZAMPA AND THE
BAY AREA BRIDGES

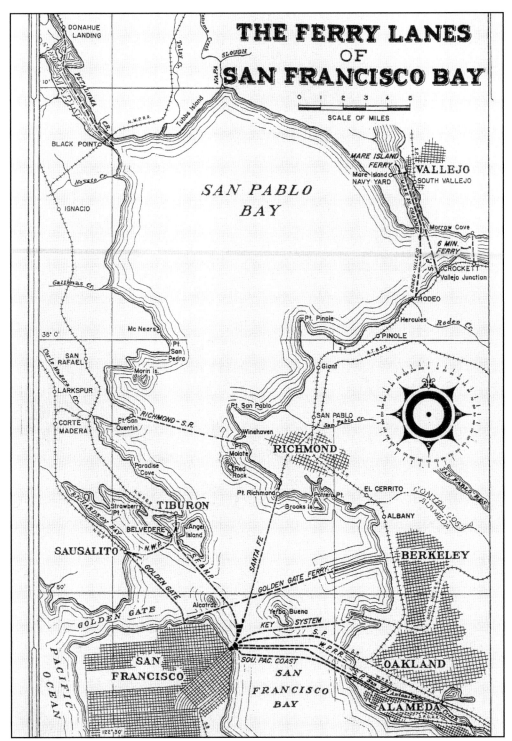

This map from around 1922 shows some of the many ferry routes that once crossed the bay. Many of the bridges in use today were built near the ferry sites because the roads, rails, and bus lines already converged at these points.

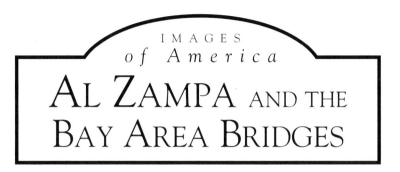

IMAGES
of America

AL ZAMPA AND THE BAY AREA BRIDGES

John V. Robinson

Published by Arcadia Publishing
Charleston SC, Chicago IL, Portsmouth NH, San Francisco CA

Printed in Great Britain

Library of Congress Catalog Card Number: 2005924972

For all general information contact Arcadia Publishing at:
Telephone 843-853-2070
Fax 843-853-0044
E-mail sales@arcadiapublishing.com
For customer service and orders:
Toll-Free 1-888-313-2665

Visit us on the internet at http://www.arcadiapublishing.com

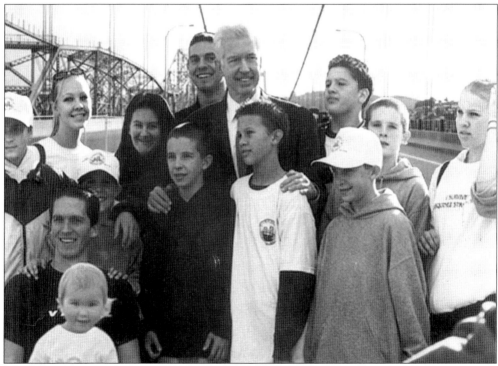

This photomontage from November 8, 2003 shows Gov. Gray Davis with Alfred Zampa's 13 great-grandchildren at the opening of the Alfred Zampa Memorial Bridge.

Contents

ACKNOWLEDGMENTS

This book would not be possible without the kind help of several people. Keith Olsen and Leo Cid of the Crockett Historical Museum helped me locate many of the historic photographs of the 1927 and 1958 Carquinez Bridges. Susan Weaver at the Crockett Library helped me by procuring rare books through inter-library loans.

From the Contra Costa Historical Society I would like to thank Betty Maffei and Lee Taylor, who were an important source of photographs for this book and provided a wealth of information about the bridges of Contra Costa County. Sylvia Dewitt at Caltrans located several rare photographs of the early bridges across the bay for me. From Peter Kiewit Sons I'd like to thank Richard Raine at the Benicia Bridge Project and Greg York at the New Bay Bridge Project for helping me gain access to those projects.

Dick Zampa, at the District Council of Ironworkers, and Don Zampa, at Ironworkers Local # 378, have been longtime supporters of my interest in their namesake and ancestor, Alfred Zampa.

Finally, I'd like to thank my wife, Lisa, and our children, Kyle, Kathy, and Ian, for understanding when I was "too busy" to do things with them. It is to them that this book is affectionately dedicated.

—John V. Robinson
March 2005

INTRODUCTION

European explorers first described the entrance to San Francisco Bay in 1769 when the party of Don Portola reached what they deemed an insurmountable water barrier at the northern end of the San Francisco peninsula. It would be midway into the next century (1846) before Captain Fremont lead a map-making expedition to the area and dubbed the entrance to the bay "*Chrysopylae*," or golden gate.

The San Francisco Bay is one of the West Coast's great natural harbors. It stretches 30 miles to the south and an equal distance to the northwest before giving way to the mouth of the Sacramento and San Joaquin Rivers. This great waterway was a natural road for early ship traffic, but the bay and rivers are a natural impediment to overland traffic such as railroads, and later automobiles.

The need to bridge the bay was recognized as early as 1869 when local crank Emperor Norton published in the *Oakland Daily News* a decree commanding Central Pacific Railroad to build a bridge from Oakland to Yerba Buena to Sausalito, and finally to terminate on the Farallon Islands 20 miles off the coast of California.

It would be 40 years before the first railroad bridge would be built when in 1910 the Southern Pacific Railroad constructed a $1.5 million swing bridge from Dumbarton Point to Redwood City. By 1910, the automobile was catching the popular imagination and soon the need would be for highway bridges.

In March of 1905, Al Zampa was born in Selby, California, a small company town on the shore of the San Pablo Bay. Zampa's life (1905–2000) covers almost the whole 20th century. He was born in the age of railroad and ferry service, worked building some the great auto bridges across the bay, and died at the dawn of the 21st century.

The first generation of bridges across the bay were conceived and built in the 1920s by entrepreneurs like Aven Hanford and Oscar Klatt of the American Toll Bridge Company, who intended to make enough money from tolls collected to pay for bridge construction and make a profit. As the automobile became more prevalent, the state bought the bridges from private interests and the long process of replacement and retrofit began. The first bridges constructed, the lift bridges of the South Bay and the Antioch Bridge, were the first to be replaced. Others, like the Richmond–San Rafael Bridge and the 1958 Carquinez Bridge, are being retrofitted to extend their service life.

As I write these words, a second generation of great bridges is being constructed across the bay: the new suspension span across the Carquinez Strait is open and named in honor of Alfred Zampa; the new Bay Bridge is progressing steadily in spite of the political and financial difficulties; and the new Benicia Bridge is moving toward completion in 2007.

In putting this book together, a balance was sought between conveying Al Zampa's story while offering a historical survey of all the historic bridges of the Bay Area. A conscious decision was made to keep the chapters on the Bay Bridge and the Golden Gate Bridge short. People interested in more detailed studies of the Bay Bridge should consult Paul Trimble and John Alioto Jr.'s *The Bay Bridge*, published in 2005 by Arcadia Publishing. Anyone interested in the Golden Gate Bridge will find dozens of books to choose from, *Spanning the Gate* (1979) by Stephen Cassady is among the best.

This book focuses on the lesser-known historic bridges around the Bay Area, with particular concentration on the three Carquinez Bridges that framed Alfred Zampa's life. Zampa started his career as a bridge builder in 1925 on the first Carquinez Bridge, and introduced his two sons Gene and Dick to bridge work on the second Carquinez Bridge. His grandsons Dick Zampa Jr. and Don Zampa then followed him into the ironworker trade, and in April of 2000 Al died in the shadow of the third bridge that now bears his name. All in all, Alfred Zampa lived a remarkable life.

One

ALFRED ZAMPA

Al Zampa is best known today for two things: surviving a 1936 fall from the Golden Gate Bridge and having the Alfred Zampa Memorial Bridge named in his honor. He started his bridge-building career in 1925 on the first Carquinez Bridge. From there he traveled around the country working on bridges of all shapes and sizes before returning to the Bay Area in 1934 to start work on the Bay Bridge and then the Golden Gate Bridge. His near fatal fall from the Golden Gate Bridge in 1936 and membership in the "Halfway to Hell Club" made him newsworthy. His recovery and return to work on other Bay Area Bridges made him legendary. The following pages offer a glimpse into the man behind the legend.

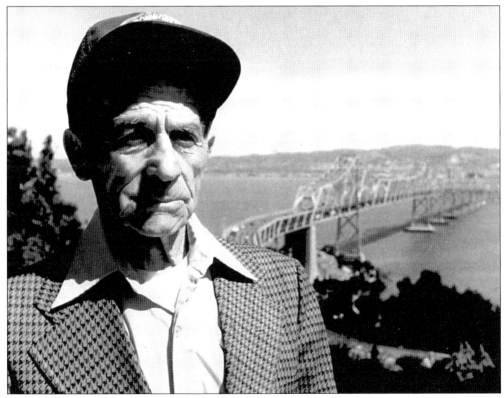

This 1986 photograph shows Al Zampa on Yerba Buena Island with the cantilever span of the Bay Bridge in the background. As the 50th anniversary celebration drew near, Zampa and the few surviving bridgeman of his era were regular features in media stories about the great bridges across the San Francisco Bay. (Courtesy Zampa family.)

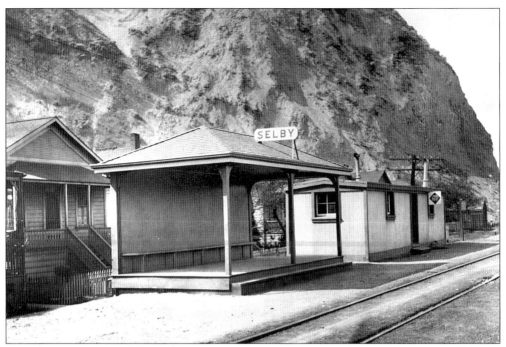

Alfred Zampa was born in March of 1905 in Selby, California. Selby was one of many company towns that sprang up along the shores of the bay during the late 19th century. The bay's natural harbor, and the waterways that extended to the Central Valley via the Sacramento and San Joaquin Rivers, made the area attractive to businesses. These waterways were also barriers to land travel and cried out for bridges. The first half of the 20th century saw a great flurry of bridge building, and Alfred Zampa was involved in much of it. (Courtesy Crockett Historical Museum.)

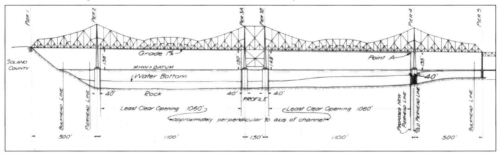

The Carquinez Bridge, depicted here in blueprint form, was the first great highway bridge across the bay. It was here, in 1925, that Al Zampa got his start as a bridge man.

> My dad told me that bridgework was too dangerous. "It's a job for desperate men. They don't care if they live or die" is what he said. But then, after he had a couple of drinks, he'd brag to his friends that I was working on the bridge.
>
> So, in 1925, I went out to the bridge and started putting in the foundations for the piers. After we got done with that, American Bridge came to put up the iron. One of the American Bridge guys asked me if I wanted to work on the iron and I looked up and thought, "If they can do it, I can do it." And so I went to work for them. That was in 1926. Now, I'd never been higher up than a garage roof before I went out to the bridge. I've always said it takes 90 percent guts and 10 percent know-how to build a bridge.
>
> —Al Zampa

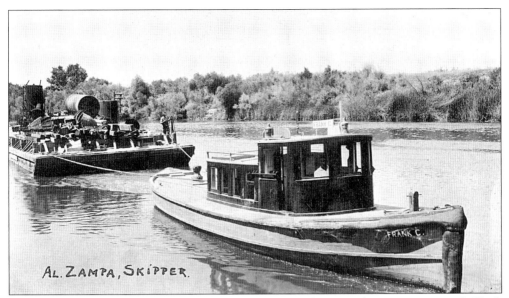

This 1929 photograph shows Al Zampa at the helm of tugboat *Frank C.* He once stated, "Back then we were called 'bridgemen' because we did everything: we put the piers in, operated the boats, drove the piles, and put up the steel. Hell, I even painted a few of them." (Courtesy Zampa family.)

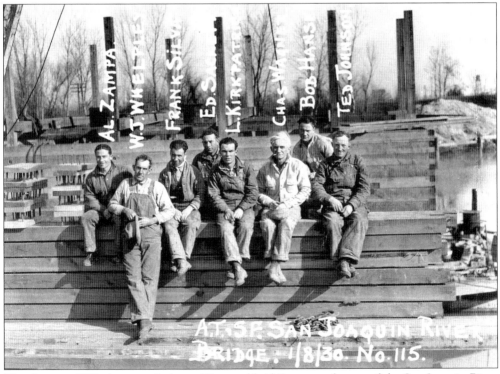

This January 1930 photograph shows 25-year-old Al Zampa and some of the San Joaquin River Bridge crew taking a break. (Courtesy Zampa family.)

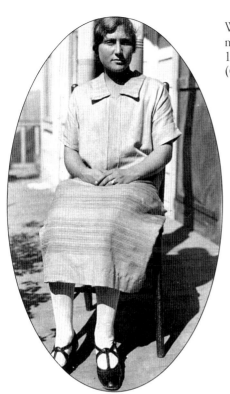

While working on a bridge near Stockton, Al married Angelina D'amico, pictured here around 1925. They remained married for over 50 years. (Courtesy Zampa family.)

In 1931 I worked out of Amarillo, Texas, way out in the sticks, you know. They built a camp there. The married men built little houses if they were going to stay a long time. We lived in a tent. I put in board floor. We had a four-lid wood stove, and I made a bed in a corner— everything, me, her, and the baby, all in a 10 by 12 tent. We carried our own water. Angelina was terrific. How many women today would move to a construction camp and live in a tent?

—Al Zampa

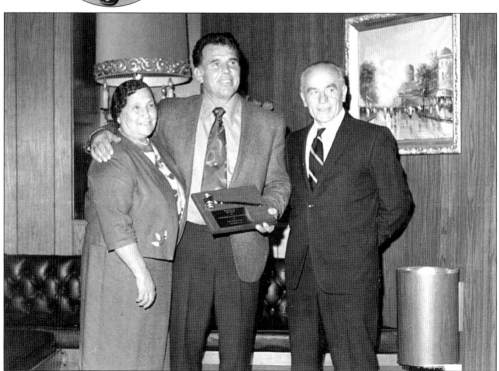

Pictured here, from left to right, are Angelina Zampa, son Art Cuitti, and Al Zampa. (Courtesy Zampa family.)

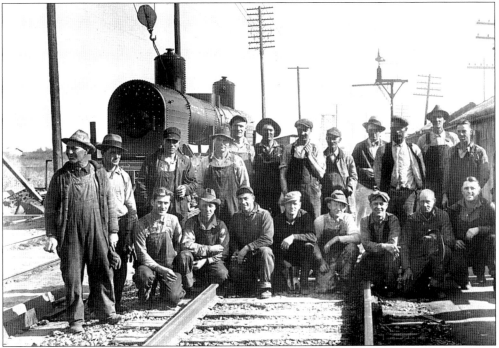

This c. 1931 photograph depicts another bridge crew somewhere in Texas. Zampa is the third kneeling man from the left. The rest of the men in the picture are unidentified. (Courtesy Zampa family.)

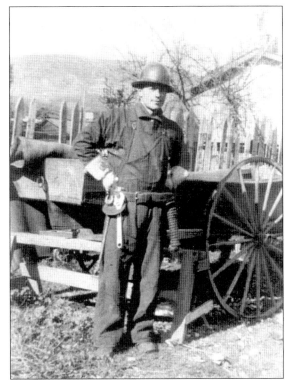

In 1934, Zampa returned to the Bay Area a seasoned bridgeman and began working on the Oakland–San Francisco Bay Bridge. In two years he would move on to the Golden Gate Bridge. This picture from about 1935 shows Zampa as he appeared in full bridgeman regalia. (Courtesy Zampa family.)

Net Grounded; Bridge Worker Falls; May Die

Because a safety net was allowed to sag until it touched the ground, a Golden Gate Bridge worker was in St. Luke's Hospital last night with a broken back. Doctors said he might die.

The injured man was Alfred Zampa, 30, 128 Third street, an employe of the Bethlehem Steel Corporation. Working on the side span on the Marin county side, he slipped on a wet girder and plunged downward.

The ground at this point is only 25 feet below the bridge span. A life net hangs under the workmen to catch them if they fall. But this net had been allowed to sag until it touched the ground and when Zampa plunged into it he struck the ground with full force.

The shock broke three spinal vertebrae and injured his pelvis. He was given emergency treatment at the scene of the fall and then brought to San Francisco.

This short news account from 1937 details the basic facts of Zampa's near fatal fall into the nets on the Golden Gate Bridge. The fall almost killed Zampa, and he was unable to work as a bridgeman for eight years. He eventually returned to structural ironwork and had a hand in constructing several more important projects before retiring in 1970.

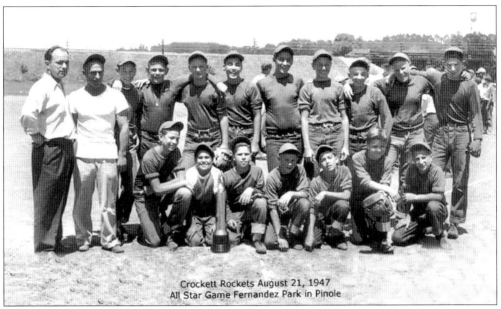

Crockett Rockets August 21, 1947
All Star Game Fernandez Park in Pinole

This 1947 photograph shows the Crockett Rockets, coached by Al Zampa who helped organize the first little league in west Contra Costa County. Pictured, from left to right, are (standing) team sponsor Tom Barbosa, coach Al Zampa, Richard Patterson, Ed Ladoucer, Joel Heckman, Rich Vargen, Vince Dimaggio, Ray Garavaglia, Willard Reid, Melvin Airoldi, and Ken Hicks; (kneeling) Ray Vallejo, Arnold Vallejo, Dick Zampa, Al Georgetti, Babe Dimaggio, Ed Zampa, and George Airoldi. (Courtesy Zampa family.)

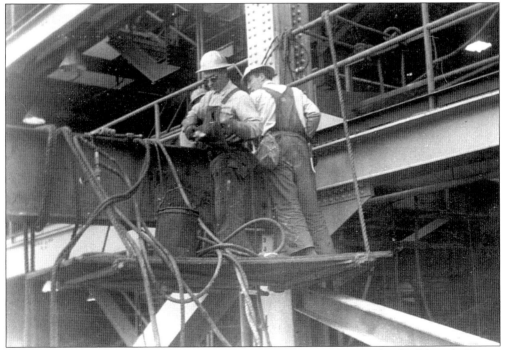

Pictured here are Al and son Gene Zampa working in a rivet gang around 1953. (Photo by Kenny Payne; courtesy Zampa family.)

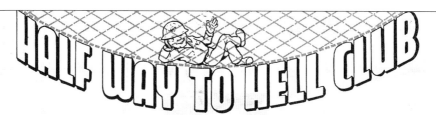

HALF WAY TO HELL CLUB

MAIL: CARE OF ERIC L. PEDLEY · 533 SECOND STREET · SAN FRANCISCO 7, CALIFORNIA
GARFIELD 1-4945

August 28, 1963

EXECUTIVE COMMITTEE:

ERIC L. PEDLEY
  Pedley-Knowles & Co.
JOHN V. O'BRIEN
  Bechtel Corp.
V. L. WHITE
  California Div. of
  Industrial Safety

SPONSORS:

ROBERT L. JENKINS
  National Safety Council
ROBERT A. WENDEL
  National Safety Council
ROBERT L. MOORE
  Lumbermans Mutual
  Casualty Co.
HUNTER P. WHARTON
  International Union of
  Operating Engineers

Mr. Alfred Zampa
Box 500 Old County Road
Crockett, California

Dear Mr. Zampa:

We were indeed glad to hear from you by your letter of August 16th. The records are clear from the news accounts of the day that you were one of those saved by the nets.

We have been trying through all available means to find any of those that were saved during the construction of the Golden Gate Bridge.

This is one of the many letters sent to Alfred Zampa regarding his membership in the exclusive fraternity of men who had been saved by the nets under the Golden Gate Bridge. (Courtesy Zampa family.)

> One Monday morning I just started work. It was wet, cold and slippery, you know, from the fog. I stepped onto one of the stringer beams. You've got to put your foot down straight. Well, evidently I didn't, I stepped out too far and I slipped. I didn't have any fear really, I figured the net would catch me and I would bounce up and land on my feet like I'd seen in the circus. Well, the net went down to the rocks. I came up. The first drop didn't seem to hurt too much. Then I came back down. That's when I had the pain. I broke my back in three places.
>
> So they took me to St. Luke's Hospital, and they jacked me up and put a body cast on me right away. I was in the hospital about 12 weeks. Later I figured I'd fallen about 43 feet. And that's how I got into the Halfway to Hell Club.
>
> —Al Zampa

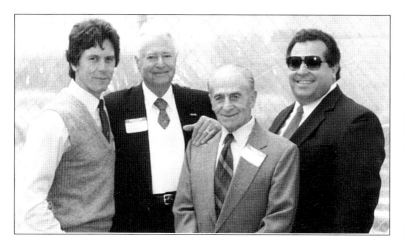

In this c. 1987 photograph, from left to right, are Don Zampa, Al's grandson; Juel D. Drake, general president of the Ironworkers from 1985 to 1989; Alfred Zampa; and Dick Zampa Sr., Al's son. (Courtesy Zampa family.)

16

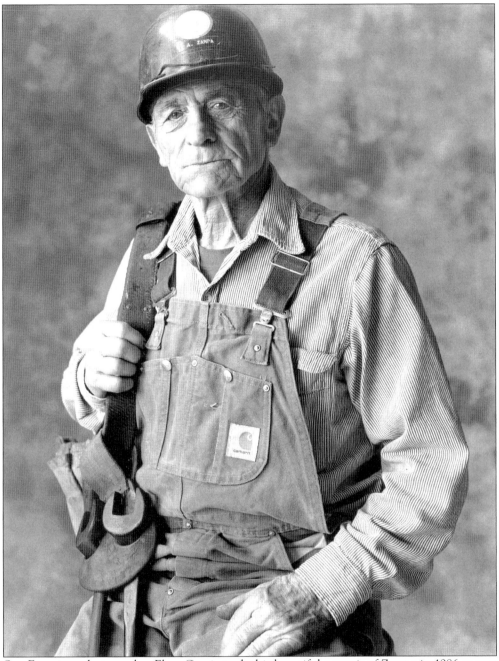

San Francisco photographer Elma Garcia took this beautiful portrait of Zampa in 1986 as part of the 50th anniversary of the Golden Gate Bridge. (Courtesy Zampa family.)

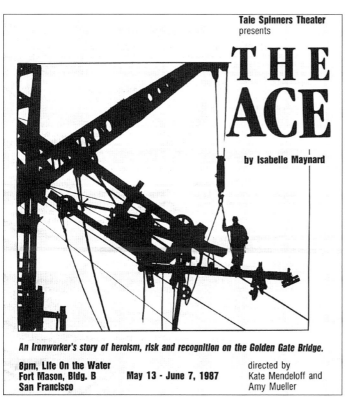

Tale Spinners Theater
presents

THE ACE

by Isabelle Maynard

An Ironworker's story of heroism, risk and recognition on the Golden Gate Bridge.

8pm, Life On the Water
Fort Mason, Bldg. B
San Francisco

May 13 - June 7, 1987

directed by
Kate Mendeloff and
Amy Mueller

In 1987, Al Zampa's exploits on the Golden Gate Bridge became the subject of a play written by Isabelle Maynard. Picture here is the cover of the play's program.

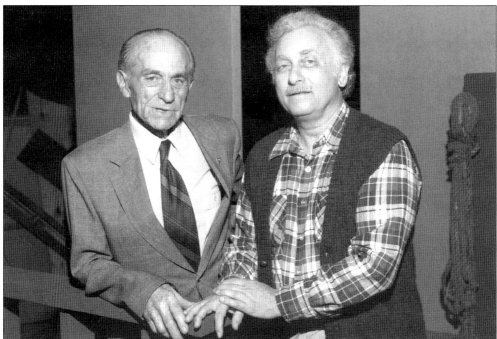

Pictured here are Al Zampa (left) and one of his fictional alter egos. Two actors played Al in *The Ace*: one as the young Al on the bridge and the other man (pictured on the right) played the older Al who narrates the story. (Photo by Bob David; courtesy Isabelle Maynard.)

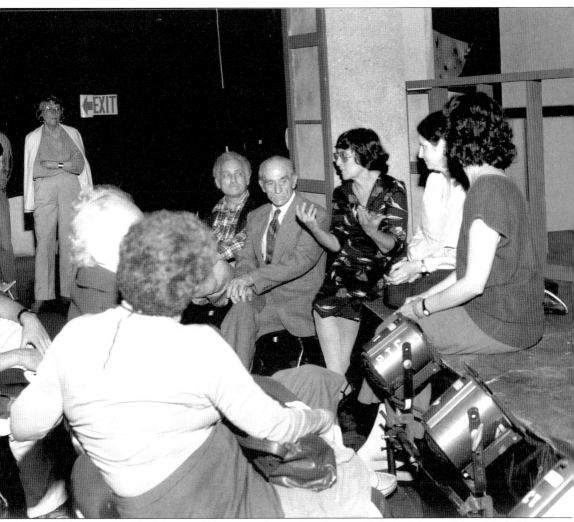

After the premier of *The Ace*, Al (wearing the suit) and writer Isabelle Maynard (on Al's left) met and took questions from the audience. Maynard said, "While I was doing research for the play I came across the story about how Al Zampa had fallen off the bridge, broken his back, and went back to bridgework. I realized the way to go with the play was to reduce the bridge to one man's experience building it. It's really a story of the human spirit." (Photo by Bob David; courtesy Isabelle Maynard.)

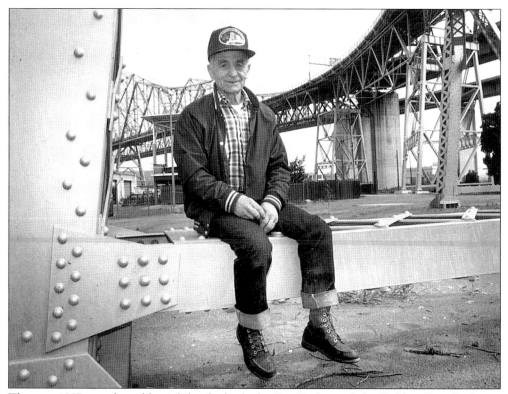

The year 1987 was the golden jubilee for both the Bay Bridge and the Golden Gate Bridge; it was also the 60th anniversary of the opening of the first Carquinez Bridge. This photograph shows Alfred Zampa sitting on the steel of the Carquinez Bridge in Crockett. (Courtesy Zampa family.)

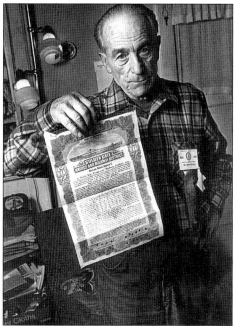

In this photograph, Al Zampa shows an original $1,000 bond issued to finance the construction of the Golden Gate Bridge. It was given to Zampa as a souvenir at one of the many celebratory functions he was invited to that year. (Courtesy Zampa family.)

The Bridge Celebration Committee in Crockett issued several different commemorative coins for the 2003 opening of the Alfred Zampa Memorial Bridge. The coins became popular collectibles. A small number of solid-gold coins were also minted.

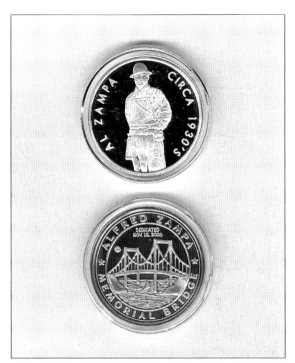

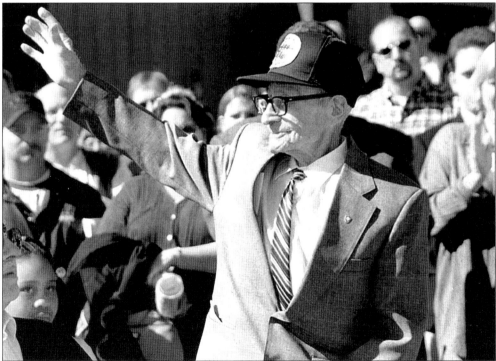

On March 3, 2000, Al Zampa made his last public appearance at the ground-breaking ceremony of the third span across the Carquinez Strait. Alfred Zampa passed away just a few weeks later and, shortly thereafter, the new bridge was officially named the Alfred Zampa Memorial Bridge in his honor.

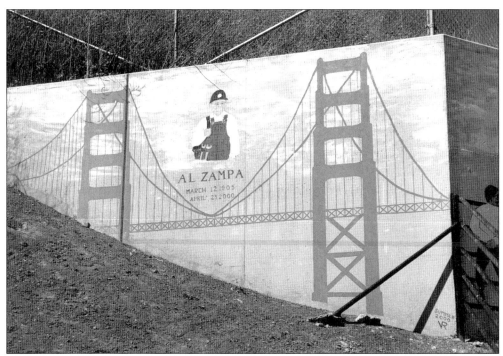

After Alfred Zampa's death in April of 2000, local Artist Vince Ramos memorialized Al by painting this mural depicting Al and the Golden Gate Bridge on the retaining wall near Zampa's home in Tormey. (Photograph by John V. Robinson.)

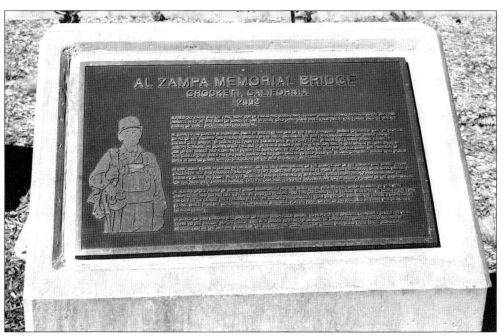

This plaque at the vista point that overlooks the bridge gives visitors a brief biography of Alfred Zampa. The beautiful setting and the pedestrian walkway across the bridge make the new bridge a popular destination for locals and tourists alike. (Photograph by John V. Robinson.)

Two

THE BRIDGES OF THE SOUTH BAY

Two of the earliest bridges across the bay were the Dumbarton Bridge, joining Newark and Menlo Park, which opened January 17, 1927, and the San Mateo–Hayward Bridge, which opened on March 3, 1929. Both were privately owned ventures and, like the Antioch Bridge that was built at about the same time, were vertical lift spans.

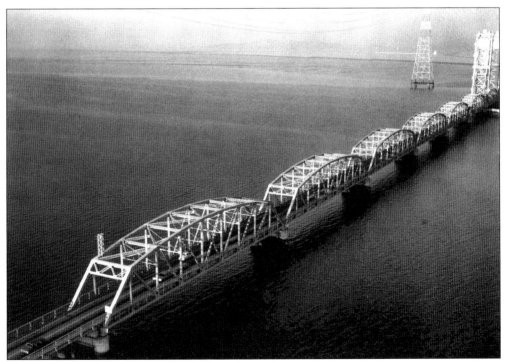

This 1975 view of the Dumbarton Bridge shows the first highway bridge across the southern portion of the San Francisco Bay. The 1.2-mile structure cost about $2 million to build and consists of eight 228-foot steel truss spans, two towers, and a vertical-lift span. (Courtesy California Department of Transportation.)

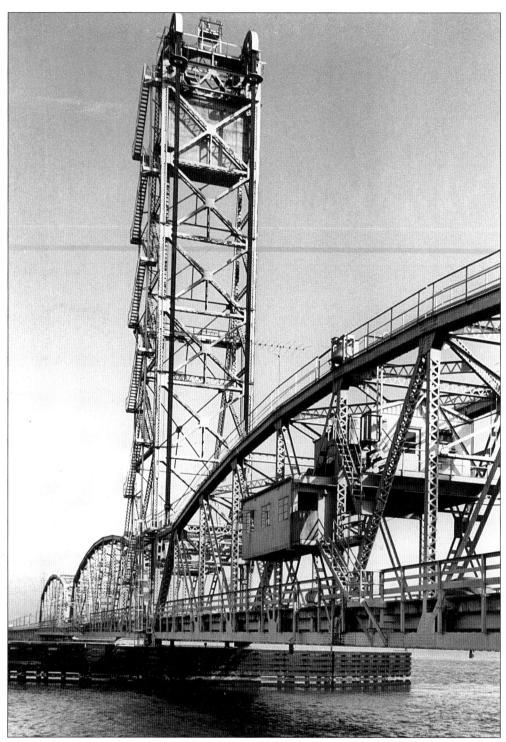

This c. 1979 photograph shows the lift span, one of the 186-foot lift towers, and the eastern truss spans. (Courtesy California Department of Transportation.)

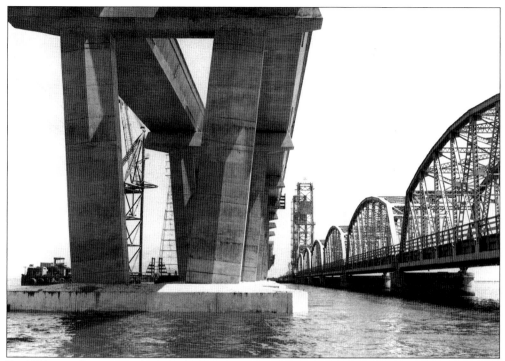

By 1979, a replacement span was being constructed to relieve traffic congestion on the older bridge. This photograph shows the new high-level concrete replacement dwarfing the older span that had been in service for 52 years. (Courtesy California Department of Transportation.)

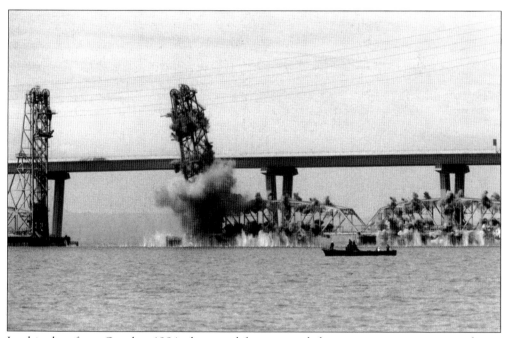

In this shot from October 1984, the west lift tower and the two west truss spans are being demolished. (Courtesy California Department of Transportation.)

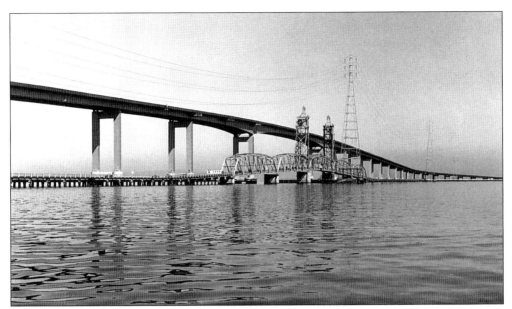

The San Mateo Bridge, pictured here in 1968, opened to traffic in March of 1929. Like many of the early highway bridges, it was a privately financed and owned toll bridge. It consisted of five 300-foot steel truss sections. The 630-ton central span could be raised to allow ships to pass underneath. By 1968, the State of California had replaced the older span with the high-level concrete bridge pictured here. (Courtesy California Department of Transportation.)

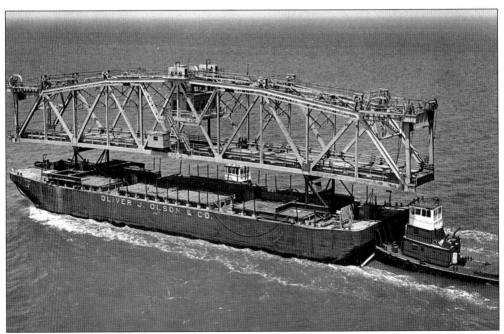

In 1968, Murphy Pacific bought the old structure at auction for $57.20 (they submitted the only bid). This 1968 photograph shows the lift span being hauled away on a barge. Ironically, it was the Murphy Pacific Company that put the spans in place 40 years earlier. (Courtesy California Department of Transportation.)

Three

THE ANTIOCH BRIDGE

The original Antioch Bridge, which opened January 1, 1926, was the first highway bridge in the greater Bay Area. The bridge spans the mouth of the San Joaquin River between Antioch and Sherman Island, linking Sacramento County and Contra Costa County. Aven Hanford and Oscar Klatt, the owners of the American Toll Bridge Company, were building the Carquinez Bridge at the same time.

The 21-foot-wide road deck of the Antioch Bridge accommodated only two lanes of traffic. Like the other early bridges, it was a private venture. The early bridge builders, for all their foresight, grossly underestimated the demands that would be made on their narrow bridges as Henry Ford made good on his boast to put America on wheels. The vertical-lift spans were cumbersome to operate and caused traffic jams on the narrow structures, so it is not surprising that they were the first to be replaced. In 1976, work began on a new steel bridge that opened in December 1978.

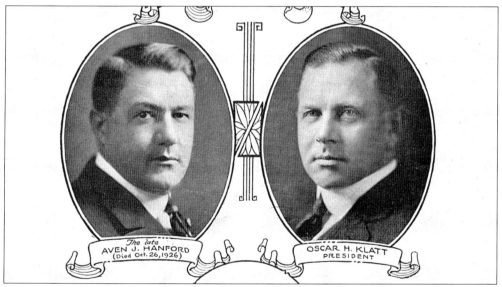

The late
AVEN J. HANFORD
(Died Oct. 26, 1926)

OSCAR H. KLATT
PRESIDENT

Pictured here are Aven J. Hanford and Oscar H. Platt of the American Toll Bridge Company. These two local businessmen saw the need for bridges connecting Contra Costa County with Solano County and Sacramento County. They financed and built both the Carquinez Bridge and the Antioch Bridge at the same time. Aven Hanford died prematurely, just months before the Carquinez Bridge was opened. Arguably it was the stress of managing these two great projects that drove him to an early grave.

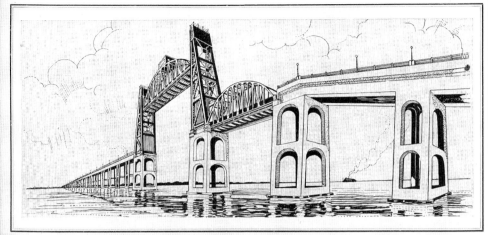

THE ANTIOCH BRIDGE

THE WORLD'S TWO GREAT HIGHWAY TOLL BRIDGES NOW BEING BUILT TO BRING INTO THEIR HERITAGE CALIFORNIA'S TWO GREAT INLAND EMPIRES

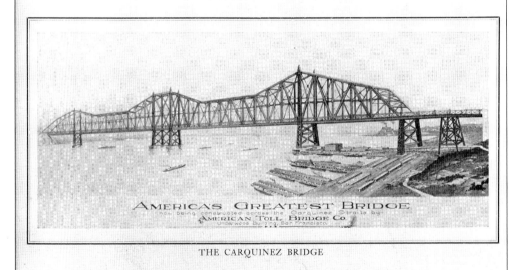

THE CARQUINEZ BRIDGE

There Is Still Opportunity to Share in the Profits of This Great Enterprise

This flier from 1925 solicits investors in the American Toll Bridge Company and promotes the two bridges that were then under construction. (Courtesy Crockett Historical Museum.)

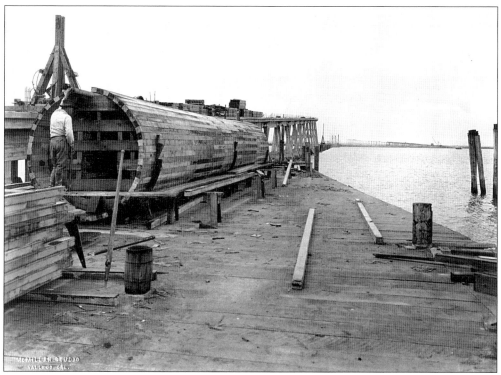

This 1925 view shows the construction of one of the wooden caissons for the concrete piers of the new bridge. In the distance the Sherman Island approach to the new bridge is underway. (Courtesy Contra Costa Historical Society.)

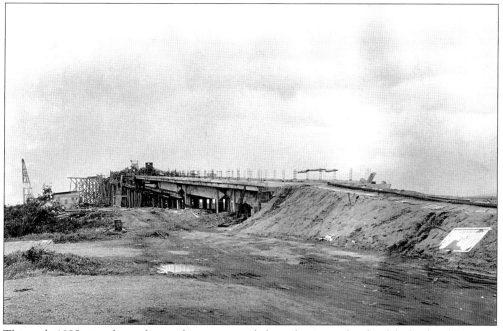

This early 1925 view shows the northwest approach from the Antioch side of the bridge. (Courtesy Contra Costa Historical Society.)

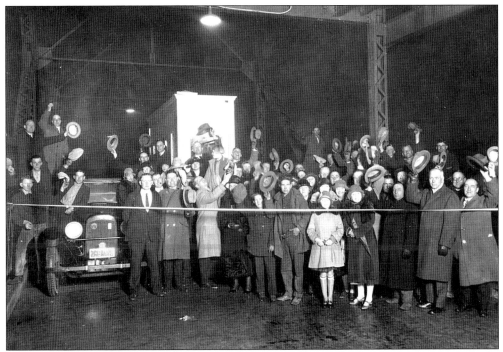

Revelers gathered to celebrate the opening of the Antioch Bridge. This shot, taken at midnight on New Year's Eve, 1925, shows the first car ready to cross the bridge and ring in 1926. (Courtesy Contra Costa Historical Society.)

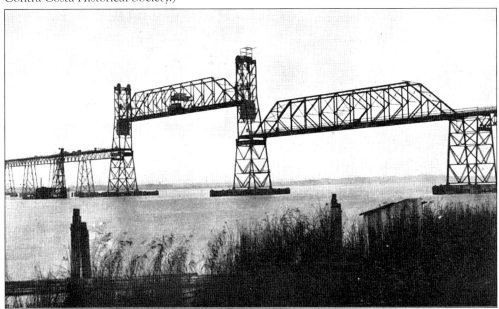

This view shows the vertical lift span being raised to full height. This 1926 photograph gives a good view of the two concrete counterweights that were employed to raise and lower the span. The disruption in traffic flow was a constant annoyance, as was the occasional mechanical failures that caused the bridge to become stuck in the open position from time to time. (Courtesy Contra Costa Historical Society.)

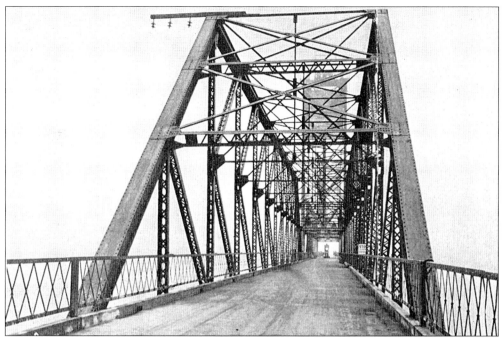

This photograph from 1925 shows the narrow road deck of the two-lane Antioch Bridge.

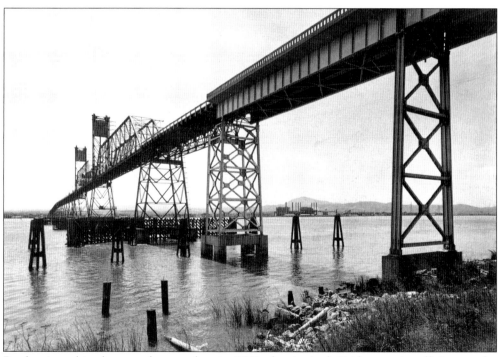

By the time this photograph was taken in 1960, the Antioch Bridge was insufficient to the traffic load it was asked to carry. Like with the older lift bridges of the South Bay, plans were underway to replace this old workhorse with a modern high-level bridge. (Courtesy Contra Costa Historical Society.)

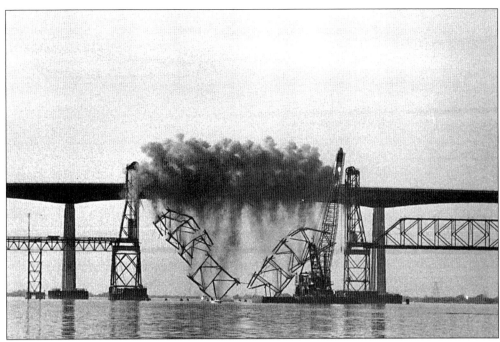

Work began on the new bridge in 1976, and it was opened for traffic in December of 1978. This 1979 photograph shows the demolition of the lift span. (Courtesy Contra Costa Historical Society.)

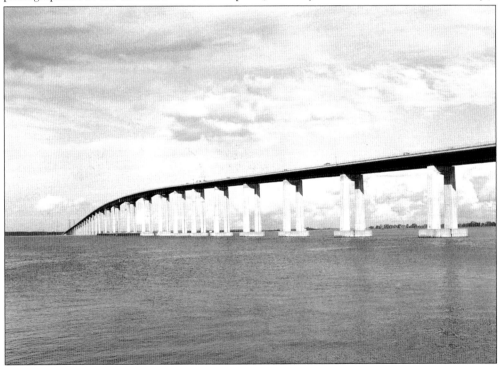

The current bridge, seen here in December of 2004, is 1.8 miles long and has a vertical clearance of 135 feet. Today nothing remains of the old structure and this graceful concrete and steel-girder span carries traffic between Antioch and Sherman Island. (Photograph by John V. Robinson.)

Four

THE CARQUINEZ BRIDGE
1927

In 1917, Vallejo grocery man Aven Hanford teamed up with a San Francisco salesman Oscar Klatt. Their mutual business interest was in finding a way to improve highway traffic between Solano County and Contra Costa County. In 1918, they formed the Rodeo-Vallejo Ferry Company to bring cars and trucks directly across the Carquinez Strait. The ferry service was a great success and long lines of cars often waited for hours to make the run across the strait.

The only practical solution to the growing demands on the ferry service was a bridge across the strait, so Hanford and Klatt formed the American Toll Bridge Company. In April 1923, work started on the longest highway bridge in the world. It was here in 1925 that Al Zampa started his long career as an ironworker. During the course of construction, five bridgemen were killed and on October 26, 1926, just six months before completion, Aven Hanford died. Oscar Klatt took over as president of the company and saw the bridge through to completion. It opened on May 21, 1927.

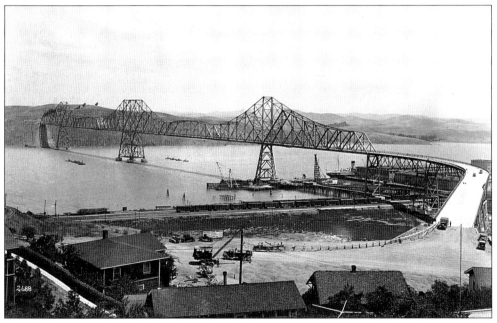

This 1927 picture shows the first Carquinez Bridge just before opening. The bridge consists of two anchor arms and a center tower. Between them are two 1,100-foot main spans with their 433-foot suspended spans that each weigh 633 tons. The total length of the bridge is 4,982 feet. (Courtesy Crockett Historical Museum.)

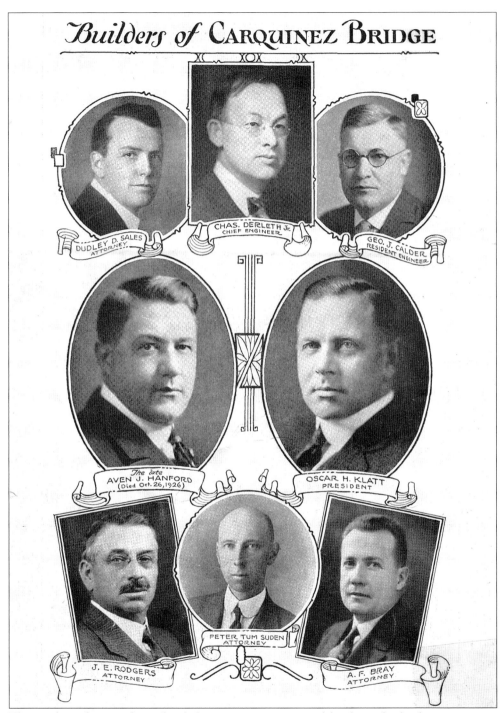

Builders of Carquinez Bridge

DUDLEY D. SALES
ATTORNEY

CHAS. DERLETH Jr.
CHIEF ENGINEER

GEO. J. CALDER
RESIDENT ENGINEER

The late
AVEN J. HANFORD
(Died Oct. 26, 1926)

OSCAR H. KLATT
PRESIDENT

J. E. RODGERS
ATTORNEY

PETER TUM SUDEN
ATTORNEY

A. F. BRAY
ATTORNEY

This is the title page from the dedication souvenir pamphlet from the bridge opening in May 1927. Along with the presidents of the American Toll Bridge Company and the bridge engineers, five attorneys are also featured. Perhaps the legal obstacles overcome in building the bridge were as difficult as the engineering obstacles encountered. (Courtesy Crockett Historical Museum.)

In this 1925 photograph, from left to right, are chief engineer Charles Derleth of UC Berkeley; Aven Hanford, president of American Toll Bridge Company; and bridge designer David B. Steinman. Steinman went on to design many famous bridges, including the great Mackinac Bridge in Michigan. The company that Steinman founded, Steinman Consulting, assisted in the design of the Alfred Zampa Memorial Bridge. (Courtesy Contra Costa Historical Society.)

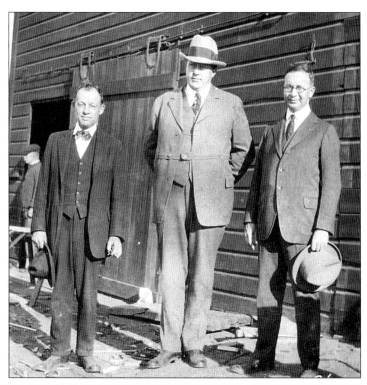

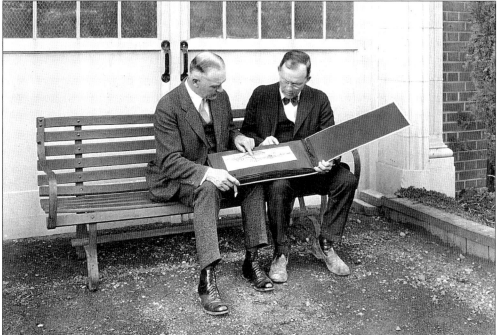

Chief engineer Charles Derleth visits the president of the C&H Sugar Refinery, George Rolph, in Crockett to describe the proposed bridge across the Carquinez Strait. Rolph had grave concerns about the new bridge being built so close to C&H Refinery operations. (Courtesy Crockett Historical Museum.)

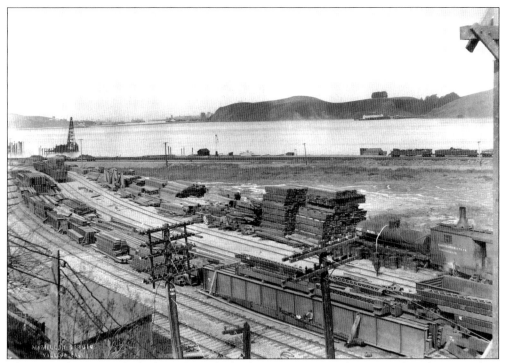

This 1926 photograph looks down from the bridge approach onto the material yard at Horseshoe Bend near Crockett. (Courtesy Contra Costa Historical Society.)

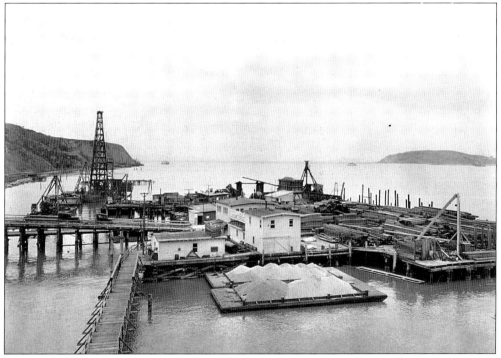

By May 1925, this large construction wharf was in place and equipped with all the materials needed to construct the massive piers. (Courtesy Contra Costa Historical Society.)

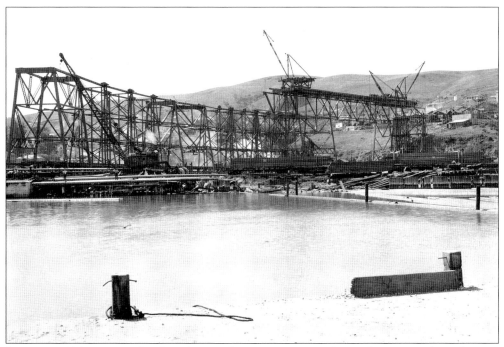

By spring 1926, two traveler derricks were busy constructing the viaduct approach to the new bridge. (Courtesy Contra Costa Historical Society.)

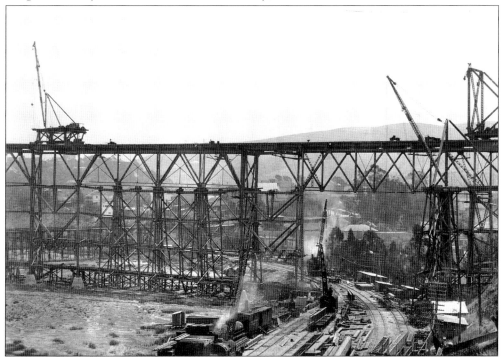

In this view from the summer of 1926, the approach advancing toward the pier 5 is seen. A large falsework support system is in place to stabilize the structure until the rivet crews secure the connections. (Courtesy Contra Costa Historical Society.)

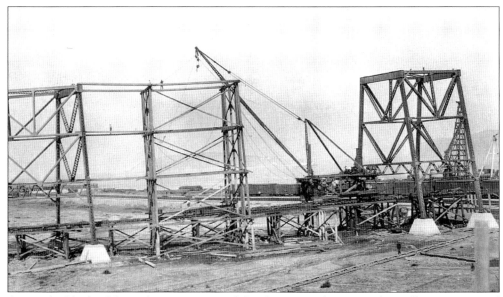

A crew builds the falsework to support steel for the approach trusses. A small steam-powered travel derrick, set on narrow-gauge railroad tracks, moved along ahead of the crews building the falsework. (Courtesy Contra Costa Historical Society.)

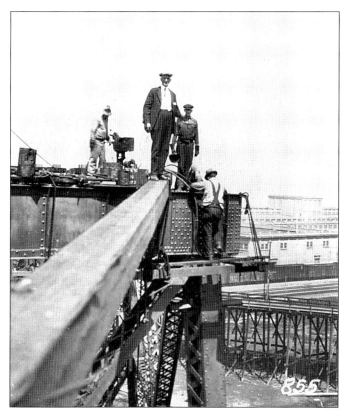

This April 1926 photograph shows a rivet gang at work. A rivet gang consisted of four men: the cooker (left), who heated the rivets in a small forge; the catcher (standing in the background), who caught the red-hot rivets in a large metal cup and placed them in the hole; the gunman (not pictured), who drove the rivets with a pneumatic rivet-gun; and the buck-up man (far right), who held one end of the rivet fast while the gun pounded the other end to a round head. The rivets contracted as they cooled, creating a tight seal. The man standing in the center of the frame is probably a steel inspector. (Courtesy Contra Costa Historical Society.)

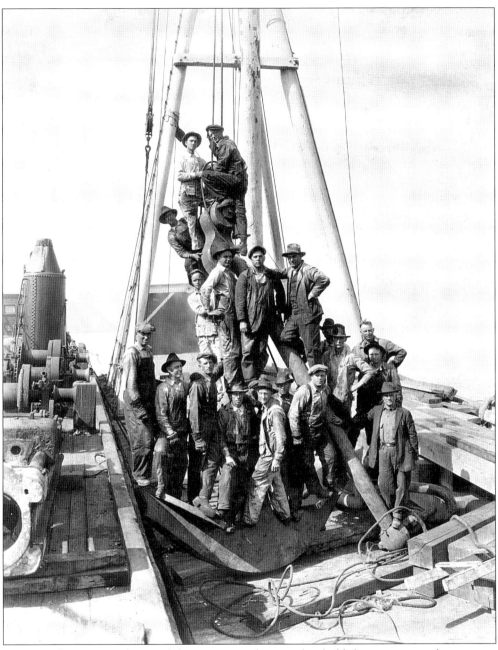

Bridge workers pose with one of the massive anchors used to hold the caissons in place against the fast-moving water of the Carquinez Strait.

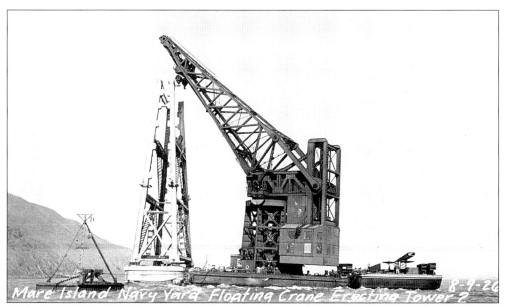

In this August 9, 1926, photograph, a 150-ton-capacity floating crane is brought in from the adjacent Mare Island Navy Yard in Vallejo. The crane was used to construct the towers up to the road-deck level. (Courtesy Contra Costa Historical Society.)

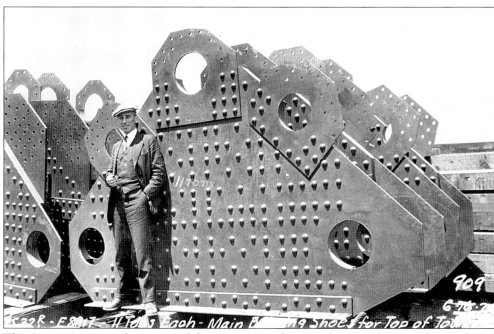

This June 1926 image shows one of the 11-ton main-bearing shoes used to cap the north and south towers at the road-deck level. (Courtesy Contra Costa Historical Society.)

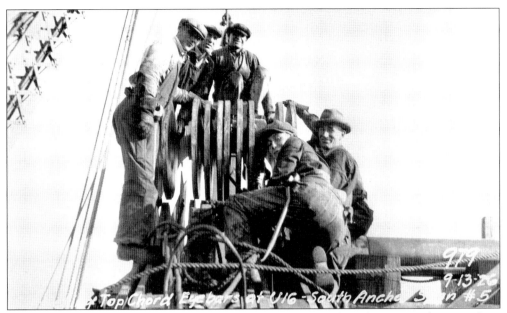

By September 1926, ironworkers had reached the top of the south anchor arm and are seen here guiding a bundle of 10 I-bars into place. The I-bars are secured by a large pin and used in places where tension forces are the greatest. (Courtesy Contra Costa Historical Society.)

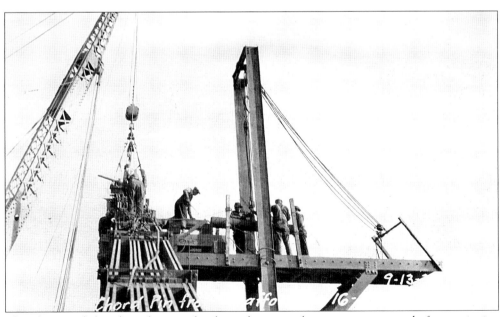

This photograph from later the same day shows the ironworkers, on a temporary platform, swinging a battering ram to drive the cord pin into place. (Courtesy Contra Costa Historical Society.)

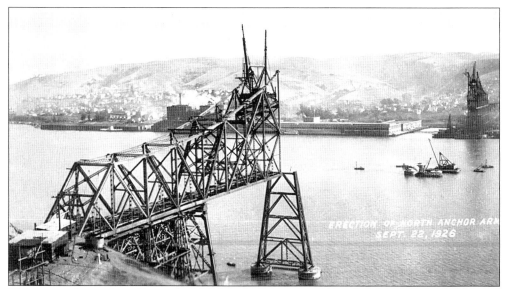

This postcard view from September 1926 shows the north anchor arm reaching its full height. (Courtesy Crockett Historical Museum.)

I turned 21 on that first bridge. I came close to falling a couple of times. Sometimes I was scared. We had no safety lines, no hard hats, and no nets. It was the hardest bridge for me because I had to do a days work while learning the bridge building trade. But the money was good. I was making $15 for a ten hour day when the guys working at the C&H Sugar Factory were making about $5 a day.

—Al Zampa

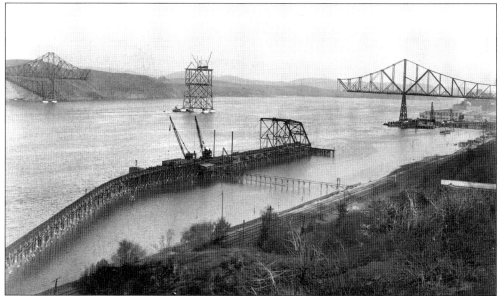

This view looking east shows the completed north and south anchor arms. The center tower is well under way, and the north suspended span is under construction near Vallejo Junction. (Courtesy Contra Costa Historical Society.)

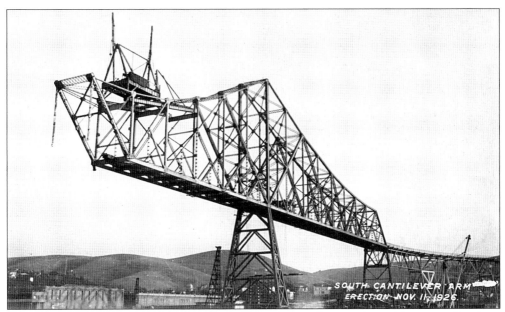

By November 1926, the south cantilever arm was nearly complete. (Courtesy Crockett Historical Museum.)

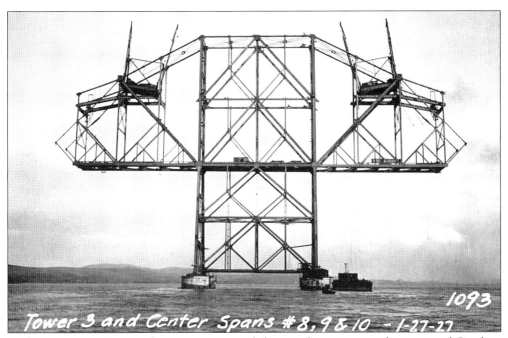

In this January 1927 view, the center tower and the cantilever arms reach out toward Crockett and Vallejo. The north and south spans were built out at the same time to keep the weight evenly distributed on the tower. (Courtesy Contra Costa Historical Society.)

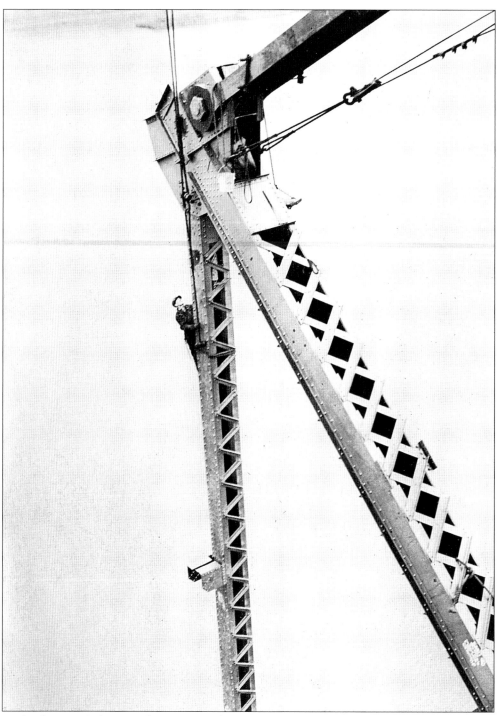

In this late-1926 photograph, an ironworker connects one of the hanger-arms on the north cantilever span. (Courtesy Contra Costa Historical Society.)

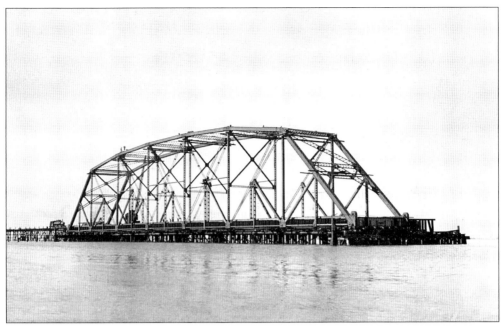

This January 1927 photograph shows the 433-foot north suspended span resting on temporary supports near Vallejo Junction. In just a few weeks, the span would be floated into position and lifted into place. (Courtesy Contra Costa Historical Society.)

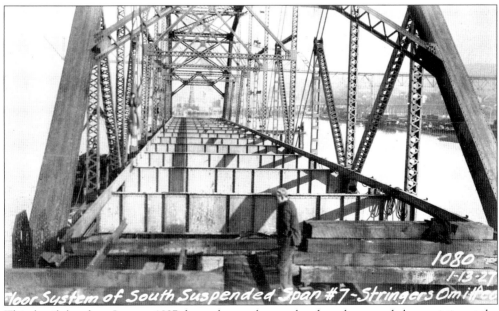

This detail shot from January 1927 shows the nearly completed south suspended span sitting at the staging area near Vallejo Junction west of Crockett. (Courtesy Contra Costa Historical Society.)

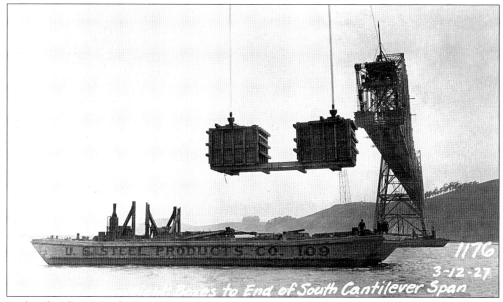

In this shot from March 12, 1927, are the empty counterweight boxes being lifted into place at the center tower. When the suspended span was floated into place and the rigging cables attached, the boxes would be slowly filled with sand, allowing the bridge to slowly absorb the extra weight. The weighted boxes would then descend to the water while the suspended span was lifted into place. (Courtesy Contra Costa Historical Society.)

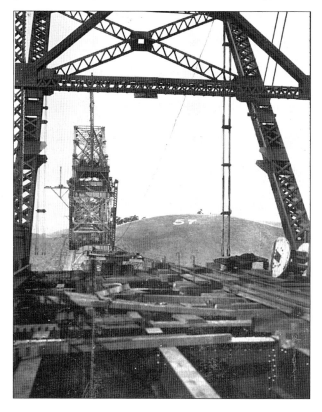

This February 1927 shot was taken from the center tower, looking north toward the north anchor arm. The time to raise the north suspended span is near. (Courtesy Contra Costa Historical Society.)

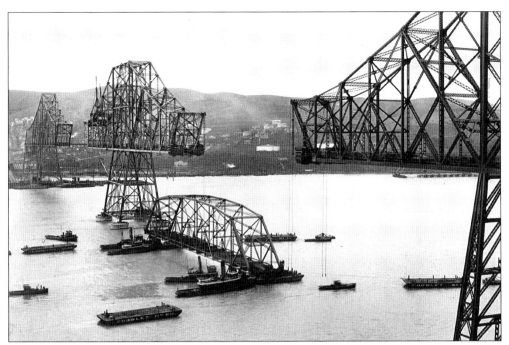

On March 3, 1927, a flotilla of tugboats and barges moved the north suspended span into place for the first big lift. The sandbox counterweights are in place and the lifting tackles can be seen hanging down from the cantilever arms. Hundreds of people turned out to watch the show, the outcome of which was by no means certain. In 1916, the Quebec Bridge suffered a catastrophic failure as the 640-foot suspended span collapsed into the St. Lawrence River, killing 13 men. The engineers of the Carquinez Bridge carefully studied the Quebec Bridge failure when planning this lift; its success or failure could make or break their careers. (Courtesy Contra Costa Historical Society.)

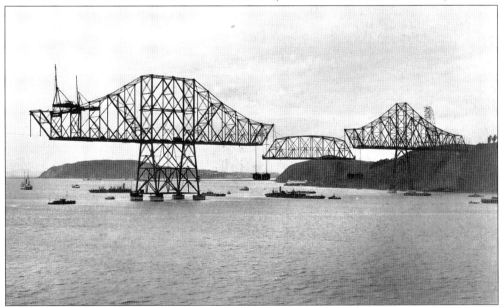

This view from the C&H Sugar Refinery in Crockett shows the north span in mid-lift. The entire lift took only about 30 minutes. (Courtesy Crockett Historical Museum.)

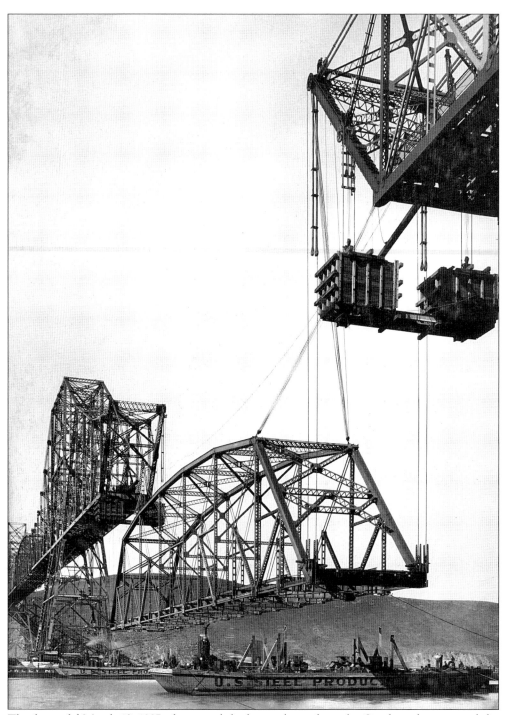

This beautiful March 19, 1927, photograph looks northeast from the Crockett shore toward the south suspended span as it begins its slow assent into place. In less than an hour the Carquinez Strait would be spanned. (Courtesy Contra Costa Historical Society.)

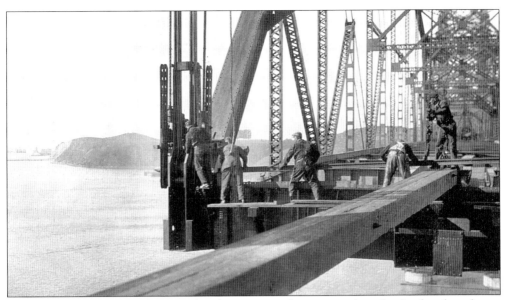

A photograph from later the same day shows ironworkers using a length of railroad track as a battering ram to drive one of the 1,500-pound connection pins into place. The space in the foreground was where the counterweight boxes had been a few minutes earlier and would be filled in with stringer beams later. (Courtesy Contra Costa Historical Society.)

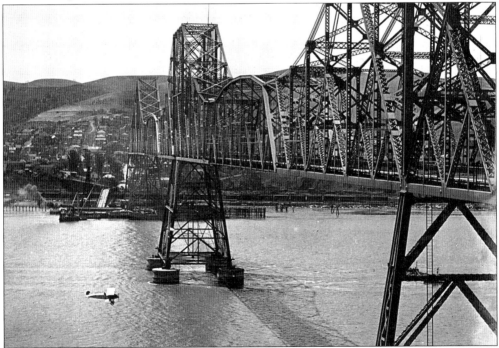

In this April 1927 photograph, we see a barnstorming pilot flying under the nearly completed bridge. C&H Sugar Refinery and Matson Navigation were so concerned the exposed center pier was a navigation hazard that they filed suit to stop the bridge from opening on schedule. They argued that a ship colliding with the pier could bring down the whole bridge and block the channel for an indeterminate length of time. (Courtesy Contra Costa Historical Society.)

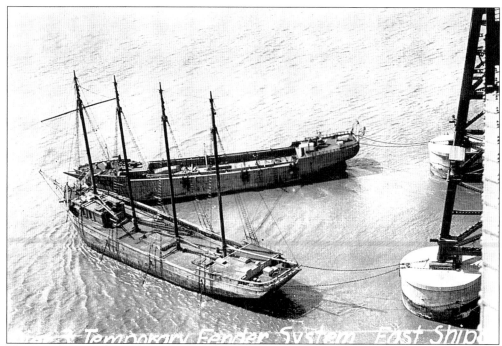

The two photographs on this page show the solution to the exposed pier problem. The American Toll Bridge Company brought in four derelict sailing ships (two on the west side and two on the east) to act as temporary pier fenders until a more permanent structure could be constructed. (Courtesy Crockett Historical Museum.)

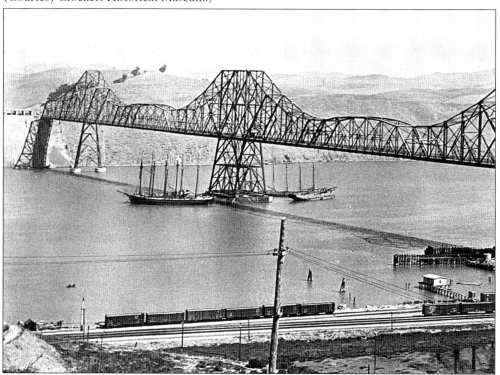

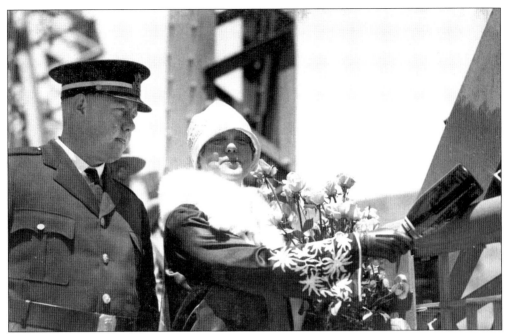

Mrs. Hanford, widow of the late Aven J. Hanford, was given the honor of christening the new bridge. (Courtesy Contra Costa Historical Society.)

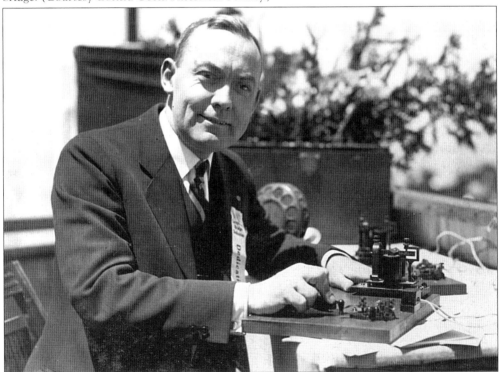

On opening day, a telegraph operator was stationed at the bridge to signal back and forth to Washington, D.C., where President Coolidge pressed a key and signaled, via telegraph, the opening of the greatest highway bridge of its day. (Courtesy Contra Costa Historical Society)

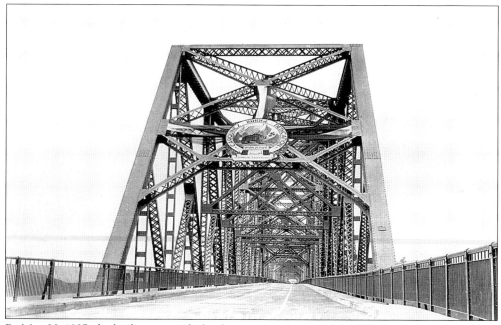

By May 20, 1927, the bridge was ready for the opening-day festivities. The bridge had three lanes of traffic; how they regulated which direction got to use the middle lane is unclear—the middle lane on the Dumbarton Bridge, for example, was called the "suicide lane" by motorists. The 1927 bridge also had two pedestrian walkways.

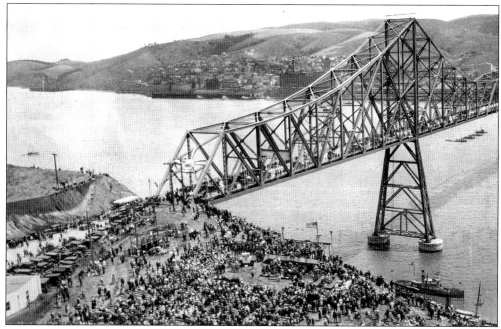

This May 21, 1927, photograph shows the large crowd of pedestrians and motorists gathered to celebrate opening the world's longest highway bridge. It was also the day Charles Lindbergh landed in Paris after making the first transatlantic airplane flight. Lindbergh's historic feat overshadowed the news of the Carquinez Bridge. (Courtesy Contra Costa Historical Society.)

Five

THE BAY BRIDGE

I started on the Bay Bridge, working for Missouri Valley Bridge and Iron, putting in the piles for the foundations on the Oakland side. You didn't have to belong to the union to work on the Bay Bridge. Unions weren't really strong yet. The Bay Bridge was about 60/40—mostly non-union men. Most of the guys in my gang were in the union. I saw the writing on the wall. I saw the unions were going to be big. So I joined Local 34 of the Piledrivers.

I worked on the Bay Bridge for two and a half years. I did everything on that bridge: I worked on the piers, I drove rivets, and I worked on the main cables. If you were good they'd move you around to wherever needed the help. The Bay Bridge is every kind of bridge there is all rolled into one. It's got the approaches, trusses, camel backs, a cantilever span, a tunnel through Yerba Buena Island, and two suspension bridges laid end to end.

Until the 50th-anniversary celebration, I'd never been across the Golden Gate Bridge since it opened. I never had no reason to go. I almost got killed there. But when I go across the Bay Bridge I can still see myself up there. My fingerprints are all over that bridge. It's a wonderful bridge.

—Al Zampa

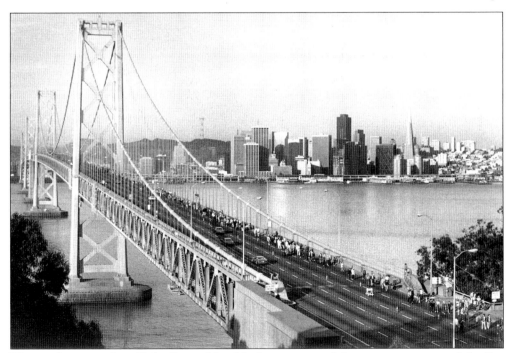

This modern view from Yerba Buena Island looks west toward the suspension spans of the Bay Bridge with the familiar San Francisco skyline in the background.

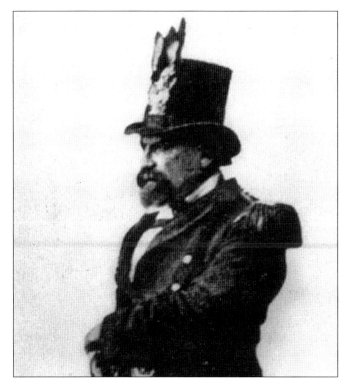

A famous footnote in the lore of Bay Area bridges is the story of Joshua Norton. Norton came to California during the gold rush and quickly made and then lost a fortune, and with it his mind. The self-proclaimed Emperor Norton The First, emperor of the United States and protector of Mexico, issued a decree in 1869 directing the Central Pacific Railroad to build a bridge from Oakland to Yerba Buena Island, Sausalito, and finally to terminate on the Farallon Islands 20 miles off the coast of California. It is odd that he makes no mention of San Francisco since he spent most of his time there and was treated as the city's unofficial mascot.

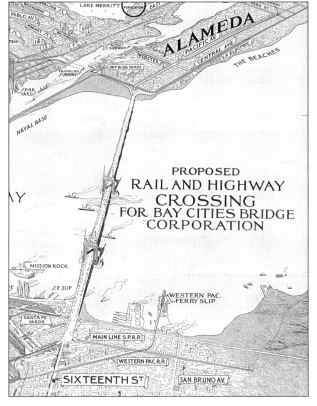

Among the many proposed crossings of the bay was this c. 1930 plan from Oscar Klatt of the American Toll Bridge Company, which had recently completed the Carquinez Bridge and the Antioch Bridge. Klatt formed the Bay Cities Bridge Corporation and pushed to build a bridge from Pacific Avenue in Alameda to Sixteenth Street in San Francisco.

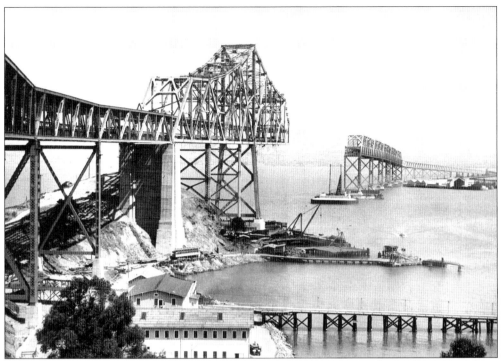

This August 1935 view from Yerba Buena Island looks east toward the rapidly developing cantilever span. (Courtesy San Francisco Public Library.)

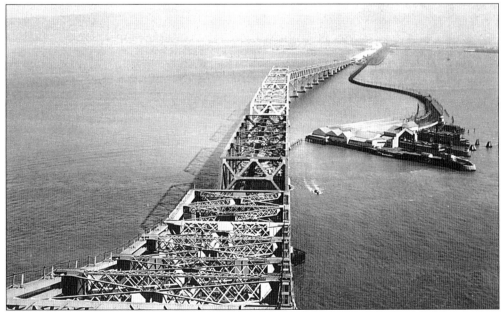

This view is from the east cantilever's anchor arm that overlooks the soon to be obsolete Oakland Ferry Terminal that was part of the Key Route System. Placing the bridge near the Key Route System made it easier to transfer the electric trolleys directly onto the lower deck of the bridge. Now, instead of getting off the electric train and onto a ferryboat, commuters could ride the electric trains straight into downtown San Francisco.

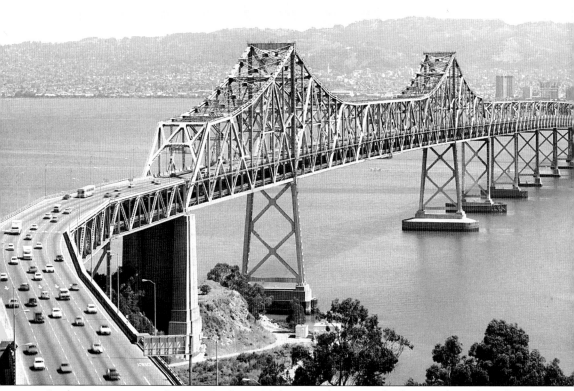

In this contemporary photograph, the 1,400-foot cantilever span leads up to the 5 through truss spans, which in turn give way to 14 deck truss spans before reaching the Oakland shore. (Courtesy Library of Congress.)

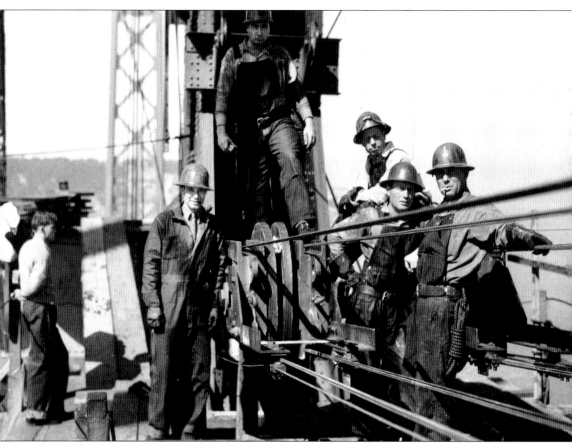

In this June 1935 photograph, a crew of ironworkers pose at the center anchorage early in the cable-spinning operation. Alfred Zampa is the second man from the right.

Once, on the footbridge, I saw a guy get hit in the mouth with a length of heavy chain. He staggered back, then down he went. He hit the water flat and just floated there. All his clothes were torn and fanned out, just like an open coat. We lost 24 men on the Bay Bridge. Whenever somebody got killed we went home for the day. It makes you think. It might be you next time.

—Al Zampa

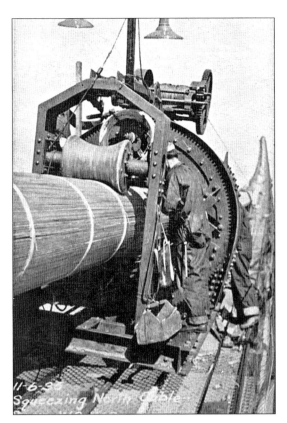

Here is one of the pneumatic compacting machines used to squeeze the main cable into a compacted, round shape. The main cables on the Bay Bridge consisted of 17,464 individual wires bundled into smaller groupings of 37 strands of 474 wire each.

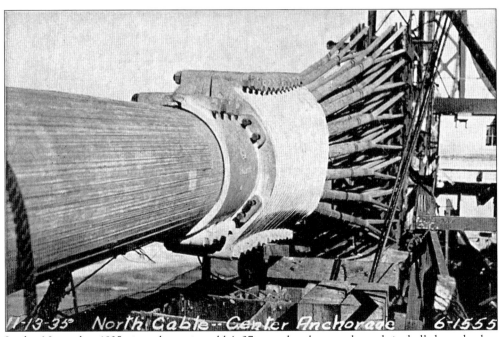

In this November 1935 view, the main cable's 37 strands splay out through its bell-shaped splay casting into the anchorage.

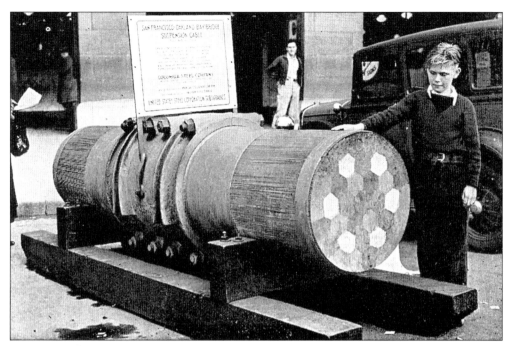

In 1936, a full-sized, cross-section model of the main cable was on display at the San Francisco Ferry Building. The diameter of the main cable is 28 $\frac{5}{8}$ inches and it contains 70,000 miles of wire that weigh 18,700 tons.

Art Elliott, an inspector on the Bay Bridge, drew the following images from 1935 to 1936. It is unknown how many of these cartoons Elliott drew, or how many have survived. The cartoons published here are from a collection of 12 on display at the Peter Kiewit field office at the site of the new Benicia Bridge near Martinez.

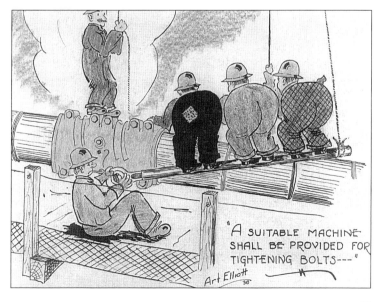

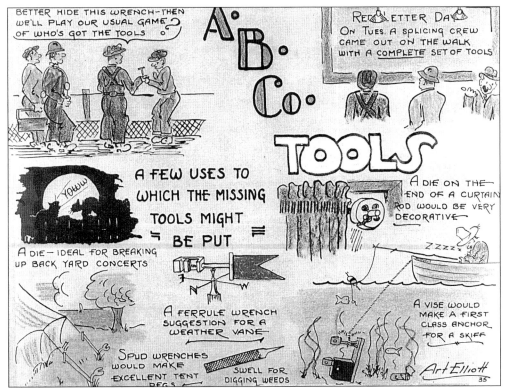

Elliott, in his drawings, often dealt with themes that are common in construction trades. In the following two cartoons, he lampoons the tendency for bridge workers to take home souvenirs from the important projects. Although, the two men depicted in the bottom cartoon look more like engineers than ironworkers.

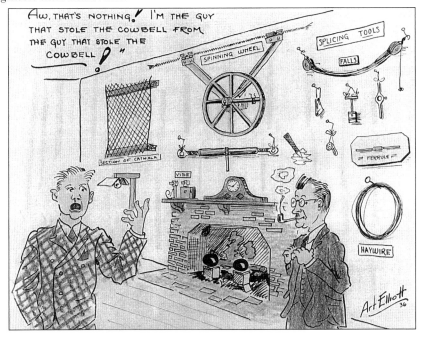

Here Elliott skewers the loudmouth boss who is never satisfied. In construction trades, foremen are known as "pushers," since their job is to push the crews to work harder.

> We made good money but worked hard for it. There was always the foreman yelling at you, 'there'll be some new faces out here in the morning.' That doesn't make you feel too good. We called the foremen pushers. Sometimes it seemed like they were going to push us right off the bridge.

—Al Zampa

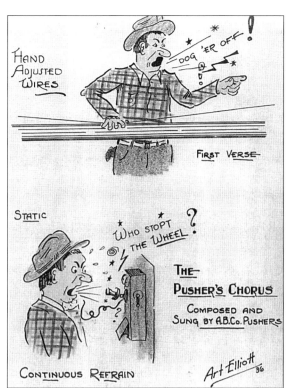

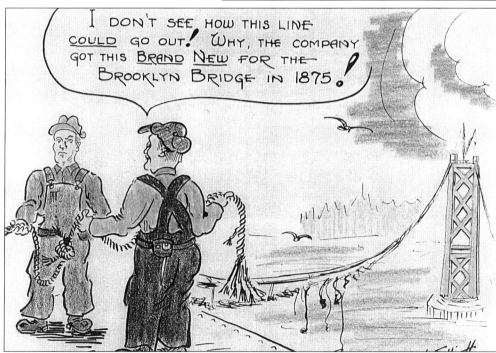

This panel from 1935 shows one of the towers in the early stages of footbridge construction. The caption may be a sarcastic comment on the quality of the equipment the men are using. It has been said, "It is the soldier's right to complain." The same holds true for construction workers.

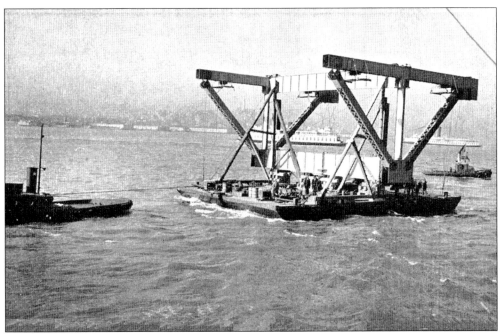

This December 1935 photograph shows a section of the road deck on a barge being towed into position beneath the main cables of the Bay Bridge. It will be hoisted into place and secured to the suspender cables hanging from the main cable.

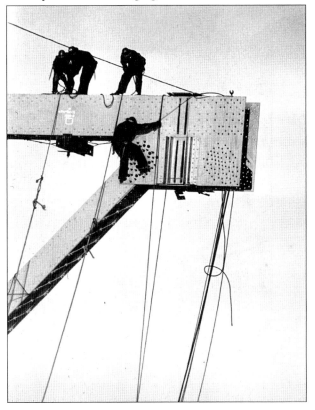

Seen here are ironworkers preparing a section of the road deck to lift into position. Al Zampa once stated, "Building a bridge is a real challenge. Not just anyone can do it. It takes a special kind of man. You can't have a lot of fear and do this job. A little fear will keep you straight though. You have to respect the bridge. The wind will blow you right off if you're not careful." (Courtesy San Francisco Public Library.)

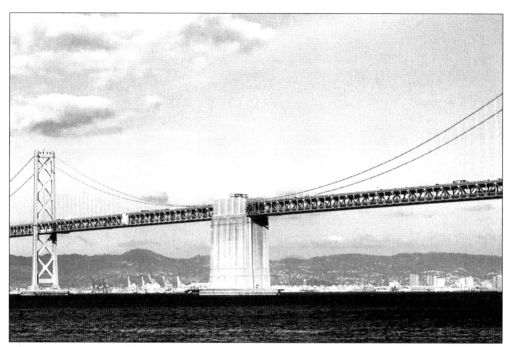

The twin suspension bridges are each 4,630 feet long. Between them lies the great concrete anchorage. This center anchorage rises 282 feet above the water and rests on bedrock more than 200 feet below the bay. (Courtesy Library of Congress.)

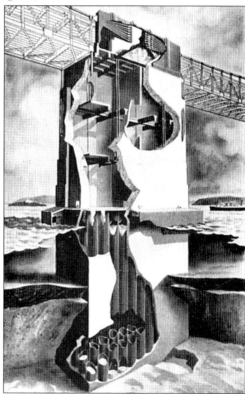

Pictured here is a cross-section of the massive center anchorage that connects the two suspension bridges. Al Zampa stated, "The center anchorage, between the two suspension spans on the San Francisco side, has more concrete and steel in it than the Empire State Building. Just most of it is under water."

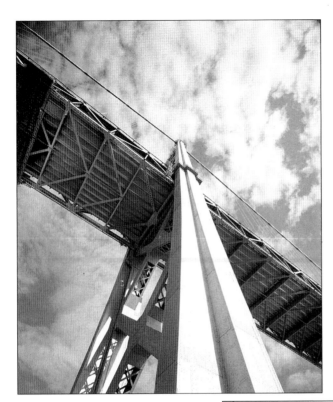

This view looking up from the pier indicates the massive scale of the towers.

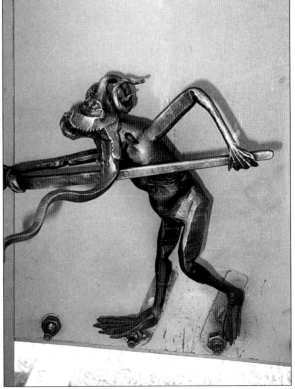

A section of the Bay Bridge collapsed during the 1989 Loma-Prieta earthquake. The bridge was closed to traffic for several weeks while repairs were made. When repairs were nearly complete, the ironworkers smuggled an 18-inch metal troll onto the bridge and welded it to the iron. It is still there to this day. (Courtesy California Department of Transportation.)

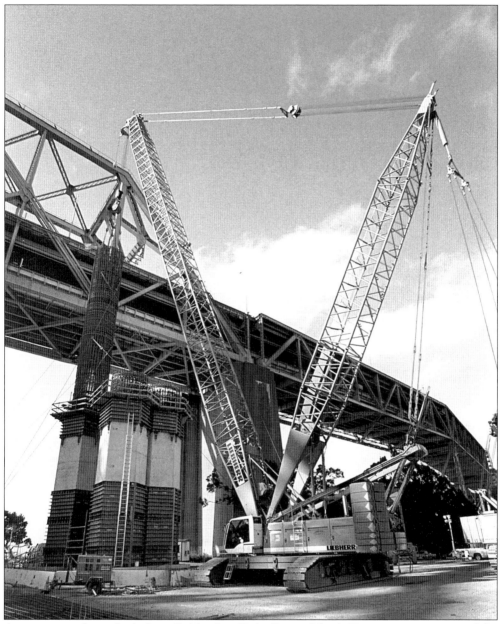

A new span is being built from Oakland to Yerba Buena Island. Here a crane sets one of the massive columns in place on Yerba Buena Island for the proposed self-anchored suspension bridge. (Photograph by John V. Robinson.)

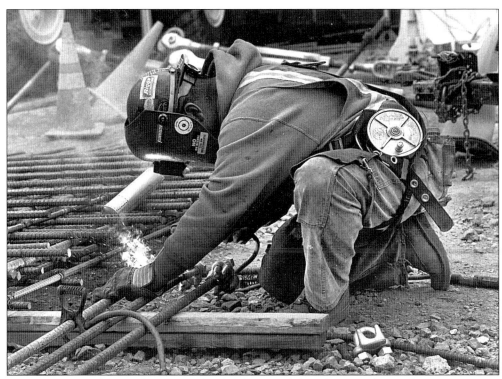

A welder is at work on Yerba Buena Island. (Photograph by John V. Robinson.)

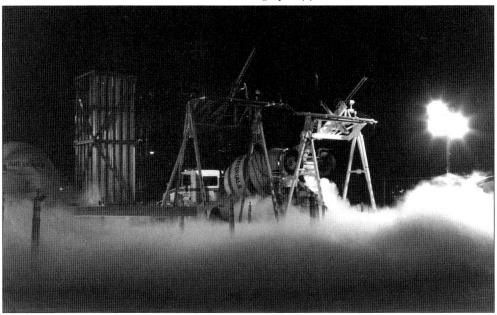

The concrete pours for the anchorage at Yerba Buena Island went on all night. In this photograph from January of 2004, a concrete truck gets its cargo bathed in liquid nitrogen. The trucks would drive into a machine that looked like an automated car wash and the liquid nitrogen would be sprayed onto the concrete to keep it cooled to 50 degrees until it could be disgorged into the anchorage. (Photograph by John V. Robinson.)

As the trucks were sprayed with liquid nitrogen, huge clouds of water vapor would billow out of the trucks and roll along the ground. Here William Kerr monitors the progress of the trucks as they move through the cooling station. (Photograph by John V. Robinson.)

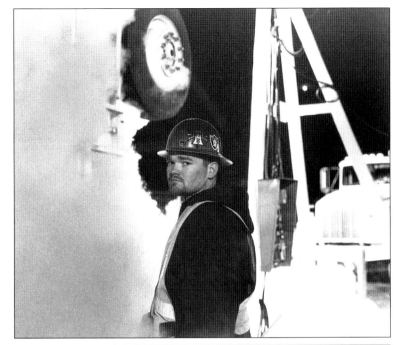

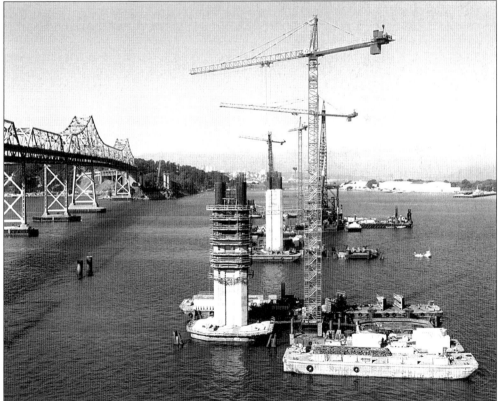

This view from mid-2004 shows the progress of the skyway portion of the new Bay Bridge. (Photograph by John V. Robinson.)

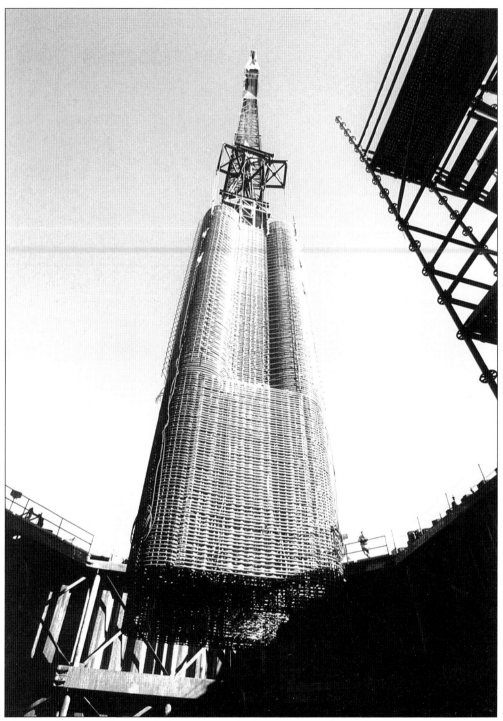

This October 2004 photograph shows one of the huge footing columns being set into a cofferdam. (Photograph by John V. Robinson.)

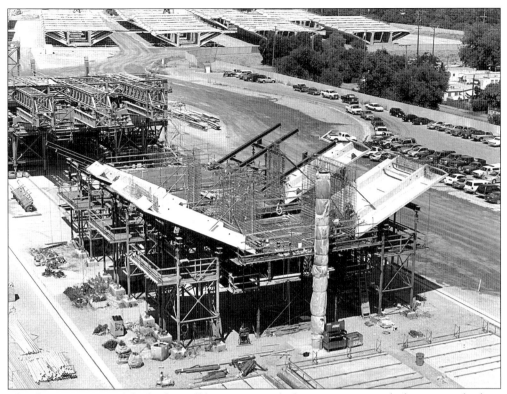

The skyway portion of the bridge will be constructed of precast concrete deck segments built in Stockton. Here is one of the segments under construction. At the top of the frame are finished sections waiting in "the boneyard" until they are shipped to the bridge site. (Photograph by John V. Robinson.)

Each of the precast segments is slightly different but they are all roughly about 25 feet long, 80 feet wide, and 30 feet tall. A straddle carrier transfers the road deck panels onto a barge where they are transported to the new Bay Bridge. (Photograph by John V. Robinson.)

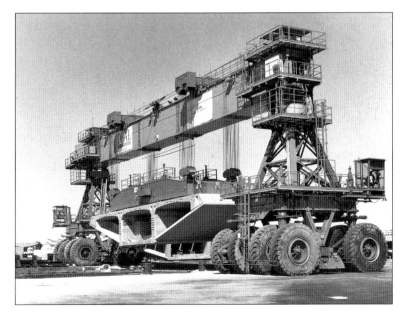

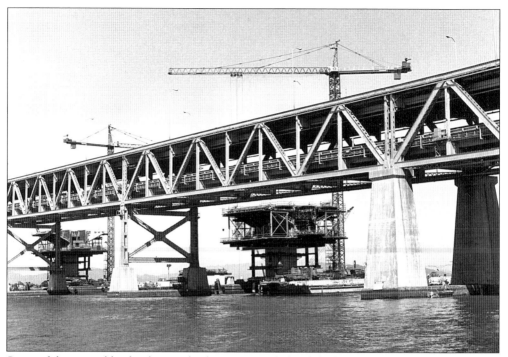

Some of the pier tables for the new bridge are rising behind deck truss spans of the older bridge. (Photograph by John V. Robinson)

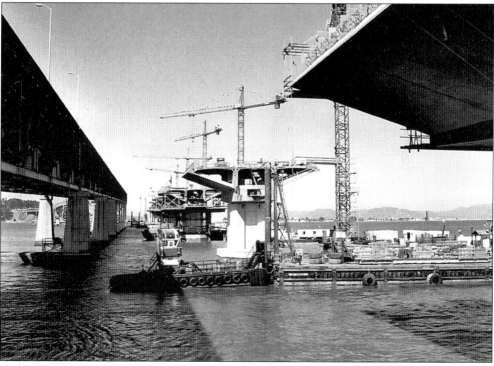

In this October 2004 photograph, some of the pier tables are ready to receive the precast sections from the Stockton yard. (Photograph by John V. Robinson.)

Six

THE GOLDEN GATE BRIDGE

Built at a cost of $35 million, the Golden Gate Bridge is one of the great architectural landmarks of the world. The Golden Gate was built at the same time as the Bay Bridge, but the Golden Gate is by far the more famous of the two great bridges. At the time of its construction, the rule of thumb was that one life would be lost for each $1 million of construction costs. Chief engineer Joseph Strauss was determined to build the bridge safely and quickly. He installed a safety net beneath the bridge as the road deck was constructed. The men who fell into the safety net formed a club that is famously called the "halfway to hell club." Alfred Zampa was a founding member of this group.

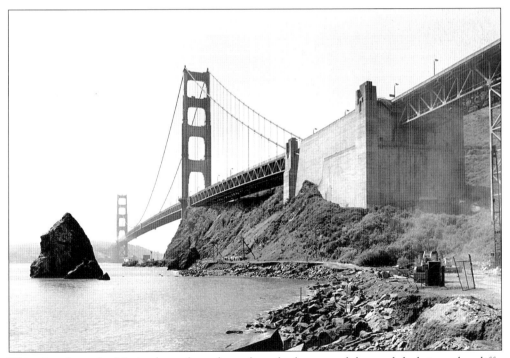

This view from the Marin shore shows how close the bottom of the road deck is to the cliffs. Because the net was allowed to sag until it touched the ground, Zampa broke his back and fractured his pelvis in a February 1937 fall. (Courtesy Library of Congress)

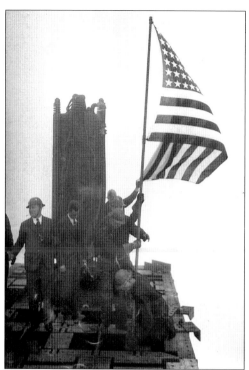

By 1934, the ironworkers had finished the north tower to its full 690-foot height. The topping out ceremony is seen here in which the construction crew places a flag at the highest point of the structure.

> *Down at the bottom of the towers and at the gates there were dozens of men waiting for a chance at a job. We could see them down there cooking beacon butts and beans in a five-gallon tin over an open fire. They'd stay there all day, waiting for someone to quit, get fired, or fall.*

—Al Zampa

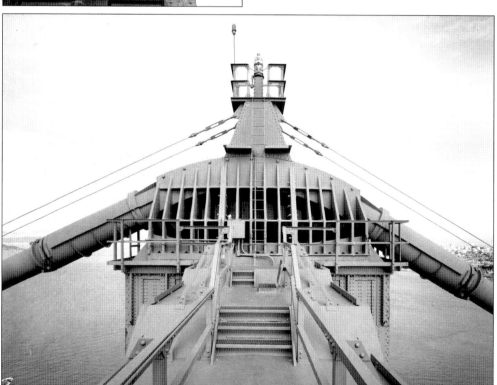

Seen here is the top of the north tower as it appears today with the saddle cap and airplane beacon. (Courtesy Library of Congress.)

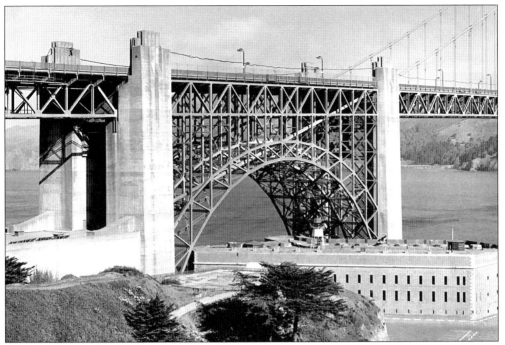

The original plan had the historic Fort Point slated for destruction. Chief engineer Joseph Strauss decided that Fort Point should be saved. This 1984 photograph displays the solution: the elegant steel arch that frames the old fort. (Courtesy Library of Congress.)

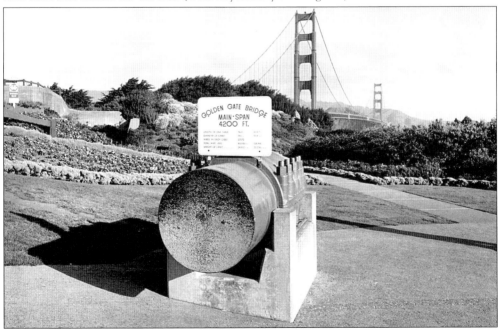

The small park that overlooks the bridge near the San Francisco toll plaza is a popular tourist attraction. At the plaza are a statue of Joseph Strauss and a cross-section of the main cable (pictured here). If there were a statue that represented the men who built the bridge, it would be a riveter. (Courtesy Library of Congress.)

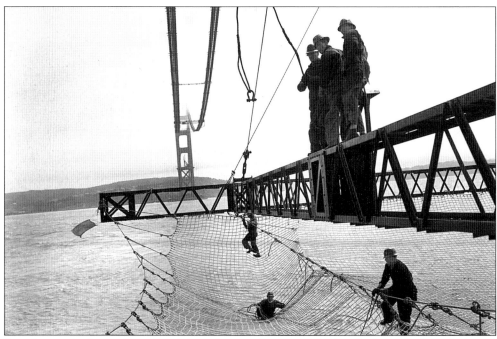

Seen here is the frame that carried the safety net. It was attached to the bottom of the deck steel and traveled out ahead of the construction work.

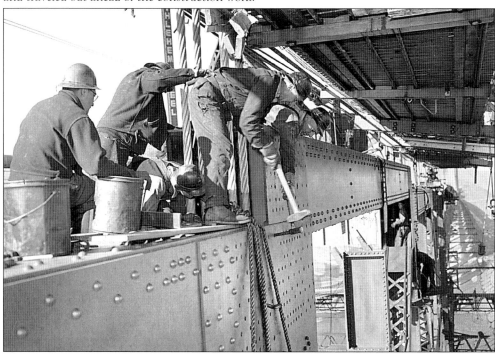

This photograph shows ironworkers setting one of the box girders in place. Note the man at the far end waiting inside another box girder to help connect the two pieces. Al Zampa, being small, was often in such precarious places: "I was just the right size. See, them beam-cords are hollow, they're not solid; I could crawl in there and buck up them rivets or help to make the connection."

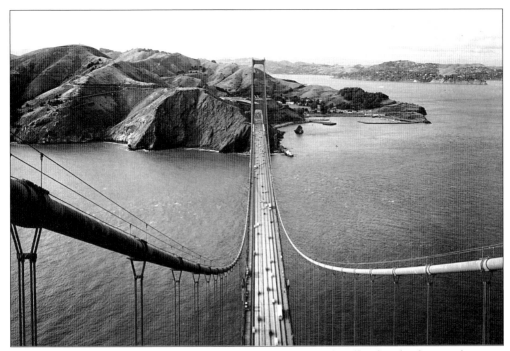

This view from the south tower looks north toward the Marin headlands. The distance between the two tower tops is 4,200 feet. (Courtesy Library of Congress.)

Here is a view from the San Francisco shore looking at the west side of the great bridge. This is the view of the bridge that ships see when they enter the San Francisco Bay. (Courtesy Library of Congress.)

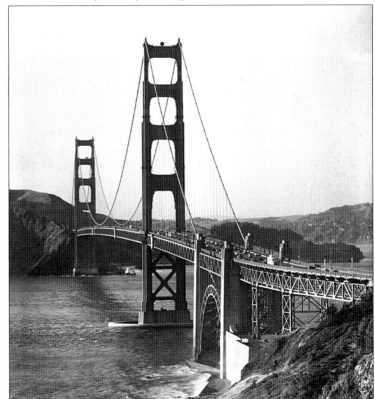

Golden Gate Bridge Fallers
Organize Halfway Club

Six young men who almost got their feet wet in falls from the deck of the Golden Gate bridge during the last several months gathered yesterday to celebrate their survival.

The six were bridge workers saved from almost certain instant death by the $89,000 safety net installed beneath the span's deck at the insistence of the Industrial Accident Commission.

Stanley, 22, of 424 Fourteenth street, San Francisco.

Ward Chamberlain, 26, of 7 Alameda way, San Ansemo; George B. Murray, 38, of 6200 California street, San Francisco; Albert Zampa, 31, of Crockett, and John Perry, 38, of 1278 Market street, San Francisco.

The last four are still in the hospital.

First notice of the halfway to hell club appeared in this article from 1937. According to Al Zampa, when a man fell to his death from a bridge he was said to have "gone to hell." Since these men had fallen into the nets, they claimed to have fallen only "halfway to hell."

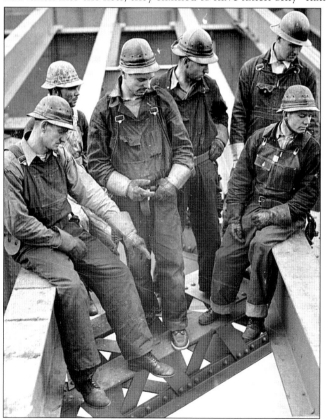

In March 1937, six of the first ten members of the "halfway to hell club" posed for this photograph. They are, from left to right, Paul H. Larry, Jack Miller, Edward Stanley, Miles Green, James Roberts, and Jack Delaye. Not pictured are Ward Chamberlain, George Murray, John Perry, and Al Zampa, who were all still in the hospital at the time. The club eventually grew to 19 men.

There were ten of us that fell into the nets those first few weeks. Four got hurt. I was one of them. We were in the hospital together. We formed the club right there in St. Luke's Hospital. People came and took pictures of us shaking hands—jolly, you know?

—Al Zampa

Seven

THE RICHMOND–
SAN RAFAEL BRIDGE

The Richmond–San Rafael Bridge, otherwise known as John F. McCarthy Memorial Bridge, spans the San Francisco Bay between Point Molate in Contra Costa County and Point San Quentin in Marin County. Construction started on the 5.5-mile bridge in March of 1953, and the structure was opened in 1956 at a cost of $66 million. The double-deck bridge consists of two cantilever spans of over 1,000 feet each, with a vertical clearance of 185 feet above the two shipping channels.

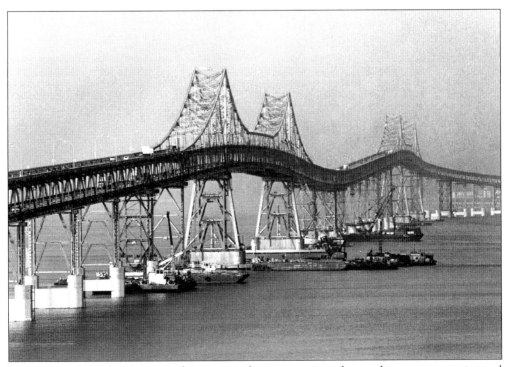

The roller-coaster dips between the two cantilever spans were designed to save money in steel costs. (Photograph by John V. Robinson.)

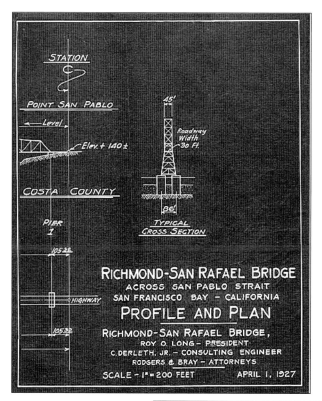

This is a detail from a 1927 blueprint. Over the years many people proposed building a bridge from Point Molate to Point San Quentin, including the ubiquitous Oscar Klatt of the American Toll Bridge Company, who was granted a charter by Contra Costa County in 1928 to build a bridge. Economic depression scuttled Klatt's plans and none of the early proposals got past the planning stages.

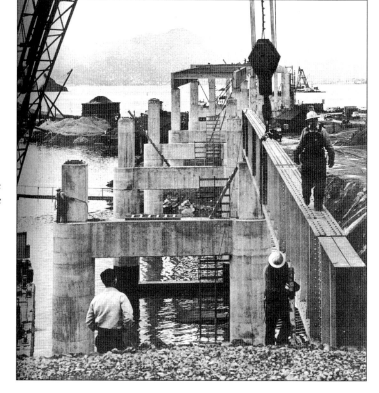

This photograph shows one of the 100-foot plate girders being set in place near the Richmond shore. The steel on the Richmond Bridge was riveted together. The age of rivets came to an end in the mid-1950s, when high-strength bolts supplanted them. (Photograph by James B. Jennings; courtesy California Department of Transportation.)

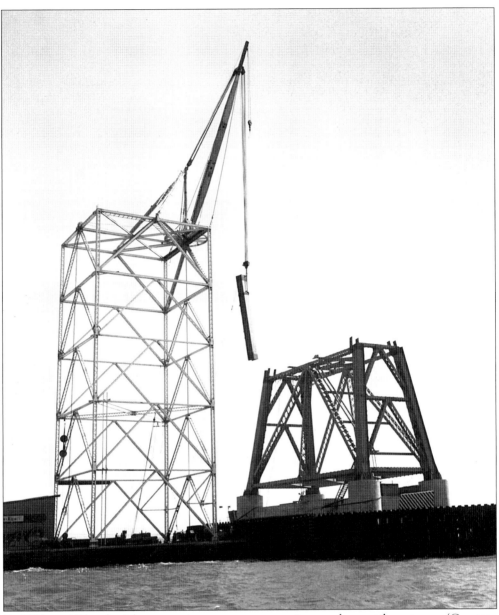

By 1954, a stiff-leg derrick was on site to start construction on the cantilever tower. (Courtesy California Department of Transportation.)

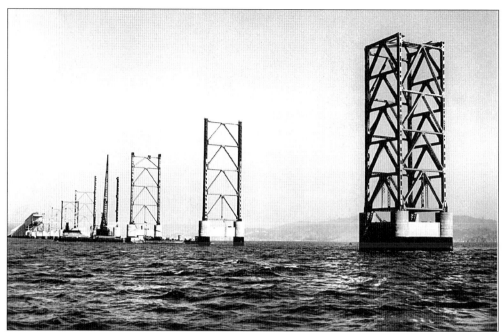

This June 1955 view shows the eastern piers of the bridge growing in height as they reach out from the Richmond shore. (Courtesy California Department of Transportation.)

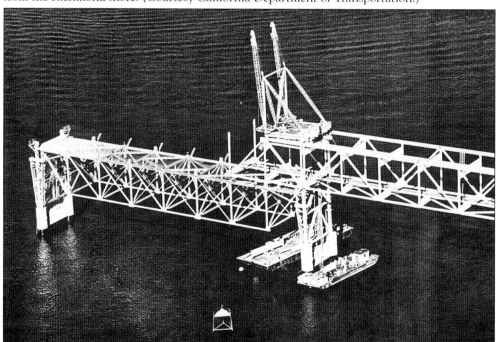

The traveler crane used to construct the 289-foot truss spans that make up the approach to the cantilever span is seen here. The frame underslung in front of the traveler is an aluminum falsework suspended between the piers. As each section of bridge was finished, the falsework was lowered onto barges and moved ahead to the next piers and the erection process was then repeated. (Courtesy California Department of Transportation.)

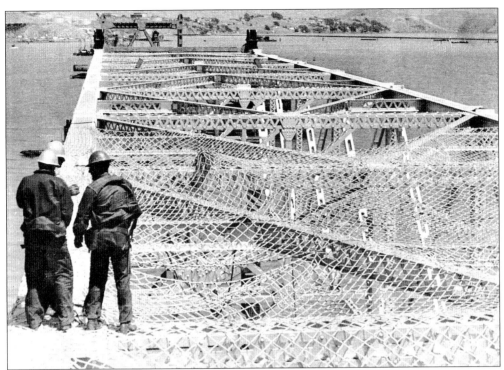

In this detail shot from the top of the aluminum falsework, ironworkers secure a safety net across the top of the span. (Photograph by James B. Jennings; courtesy California Department of Transportation.)

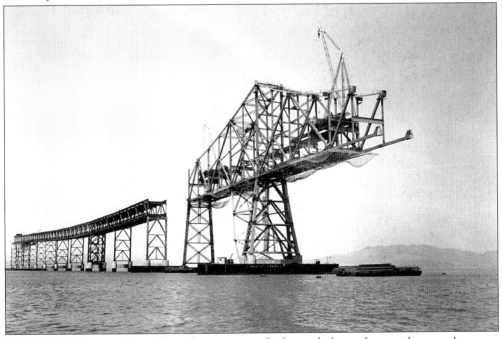

This view, looking northwest from the water near Richmond, shows the cantilever anchor arms under construction. (Courtesy California Department of Transportation.)

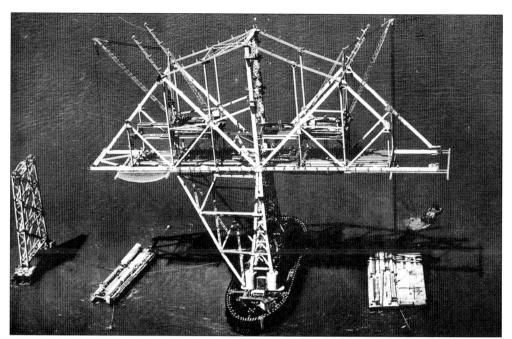

This southerly view displays the cantilever anchor arms under construction. The diagonal brace coming up from the pier was used to help support the traveler crane during the early stages of the anchor arm's construction. (Photograph by James B. Jennings; courtesy California Department of Transportation.)

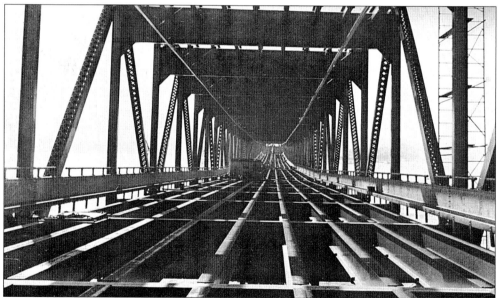

This c. 1954 view shows the steelwork of the lower deck of the bridge; the bridge was scheduled to be built in two stages. First the upper deck was to be opened to two-way traffic, and then (when extra money was at hand) the lower deck would be finished as late as 1967. Fortunately, Gov. Goodwin Knight secured the extra money and stage two was completed just a year after the bridge's opening. (Photograph by James B. Jennings; courtesy California Department of Transportation.)

Eight

THE CARQUINEZ BRIDGE
1958

By the end of the 1940s, traffic congestion on the 1927 Carquinez Bridge had reached a point where plans were made to build a parallel structure. The second bridge, a cantilever and near twin of the first, was started in 1955 and opened for traffic in November 1958. The overall project was a part of the newly developed Interstate Highway System. It was on the second Carquinez Bridge that Al Zampa had the satisfaction of working alongside his two sons Gene and Dick.

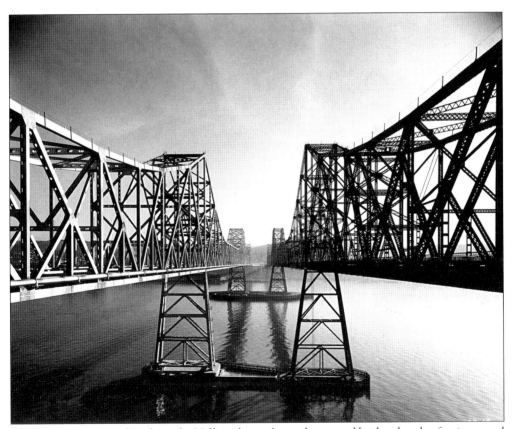

This southerly view, taken from the Vallejo shore, shows the second bridge shortly after it opened in 1958, with its the near-twin older sibling.

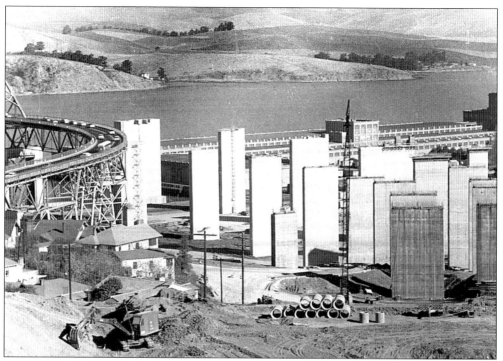

In this view looking north form Crockett are the massive cement piers for the approach to the new bridge. These giant cement panels were called "the tombstones" by local residents. (Courtesy Crockett Historical Museum.)

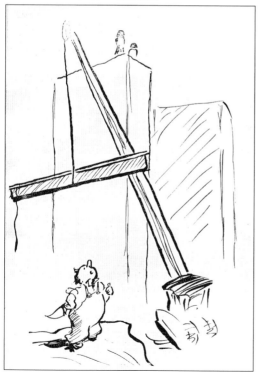

Watching a construction project is a popular pedestrian activity. Spectators are called "sidewalk superintendents" in the construction industry. In April 1957, the C&H publication *Cublet Press* ran this cartoon with a caption reminding people to watch the action from a safe distance. (Courtesy Crockett Historical Museum.)

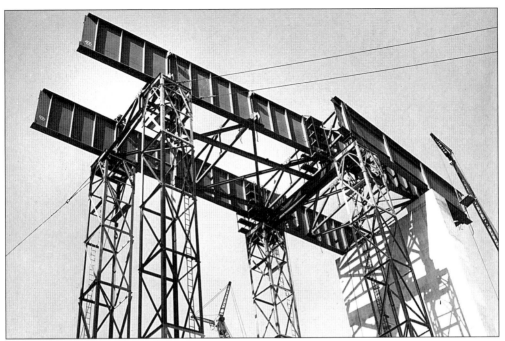

A series of long girders were used to span the distance between the concrete piers of the bridge approach. (Courtesy Crockett Historical Museum.)

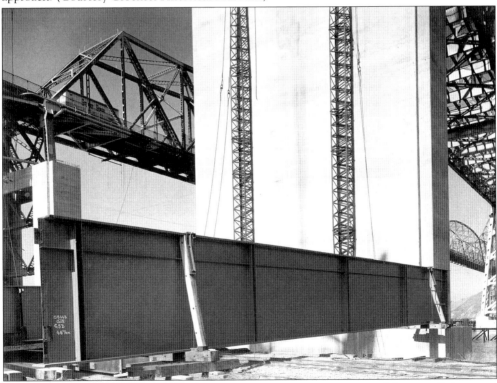

Once the girders were in place atop the piers, temporary towers supported them until they were securely bolted. (Courtesy Crockett Historical Museum.)

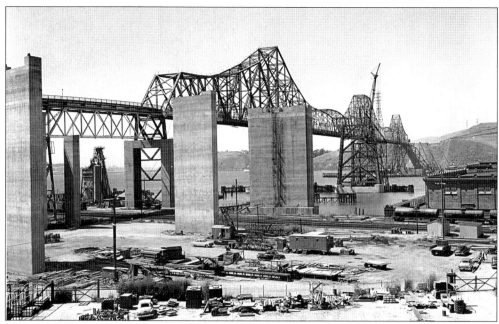

This July 1957 view, looking north from the Crockett shore, shows the south anchor-arm tower beginning to take shape. (Courtesy Vallejo Navel Museum.)

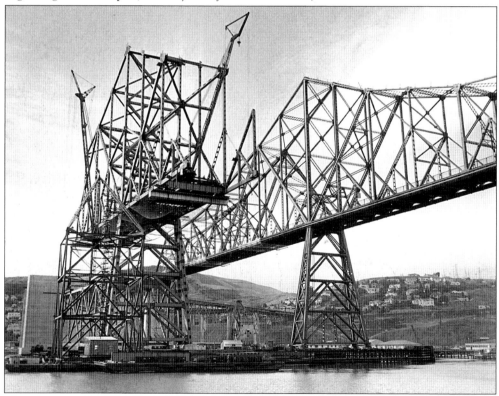

This photograph, taken a few weeks later, shows that the construction of the south anchor arm is progressing nicely. (Courtesy California Department of Transportation.)

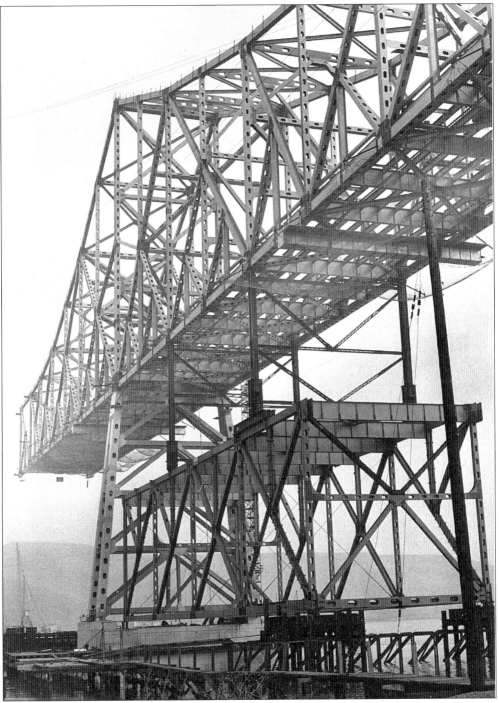

This photograph from August 1957 displays the nearly completed south anchor arm. A 247-foot section of steel falsework is visible beneath the span. It was later barged over to the north shore and served the same function for the north anchor arm. Eventually, the 500 tons of steel would be dismantled and used to connect the center tower to the north and south anchor arms. (Courtesy California Department of Transportation.)

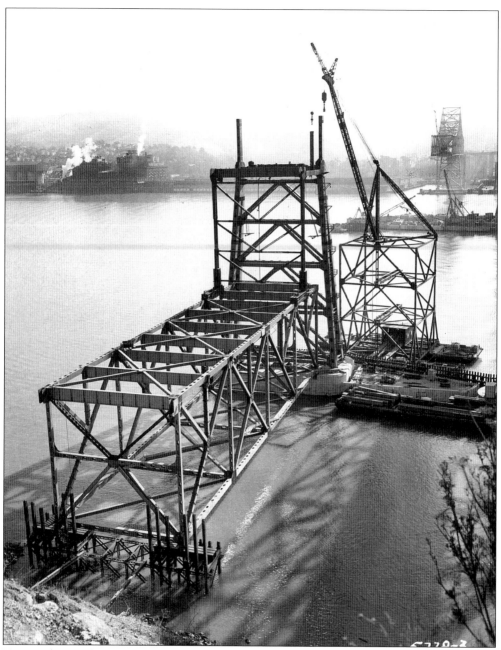

Here is the north anchor arm taking shape near the Vallejo shore. The erection span is in place to act as a temporary falsework. Once the anchor arm was complete, the erection span was dismantled and the steel was used to fill in the middle of the span. (Courtesy California Department of Transportation.)

In August 1958, the steelwork was reaching out from the center pier toward the south anchor arm. The bridge would be ready for traffic in just three months. (Courtesy California Department of Transportation.)

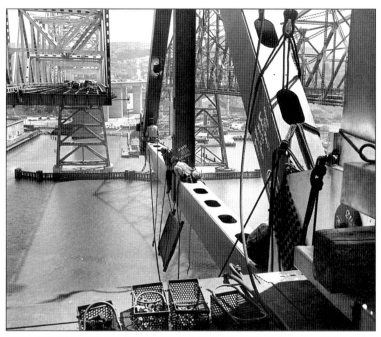

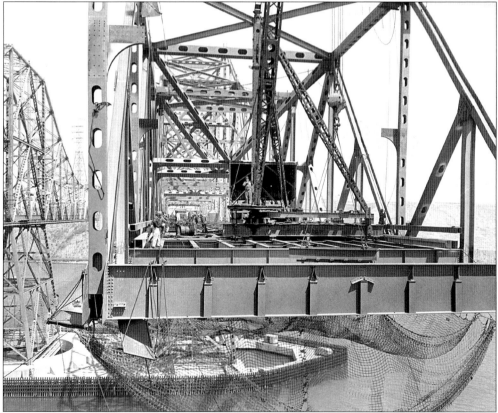

This view looks north from the south anchor arm as the road deck nears completion in August 1958. (Courtesy California Department of Transportation.)

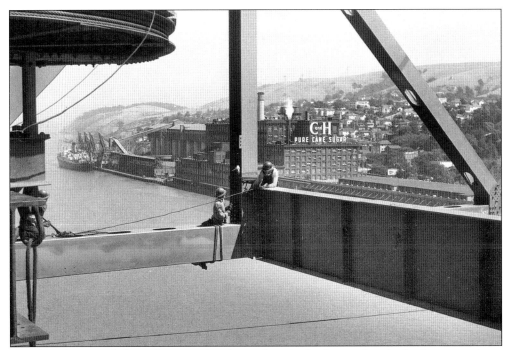

Another photograph from the same day shows that the bridge workers had a fine view down the Carquinez Strait. The C&H Sugar Refinery is visible in the distance. (Courtesy California Department of Transportation.)

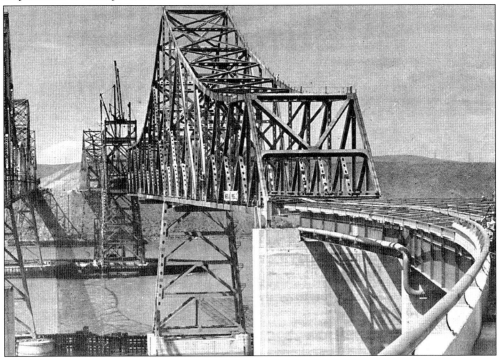

By the spring of 1958, the two anchor arms are complete and the center tower is well under way. (Courtesy California Department of Transportation.)

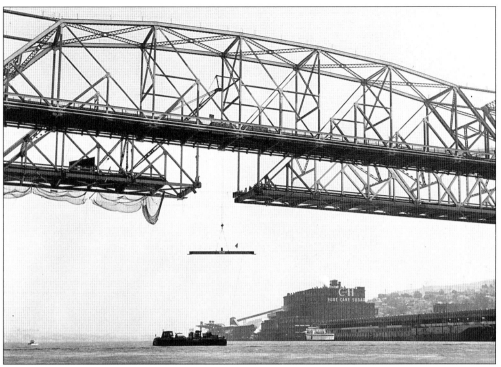

In this 1958 photograph, one of the final beams is being lifted into place. It is adorned with a flag in the manner of a topping-out ceremony. (Courtesy California Department of Transportation.)

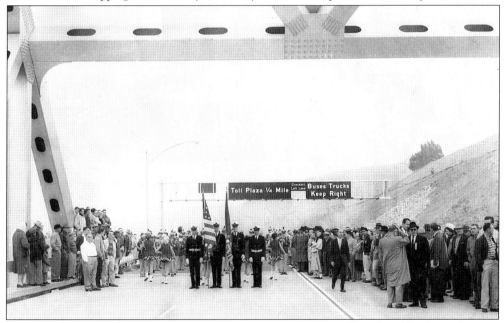

Opening day November 25, 1958, saw a color guard and a marching band lead a pedestrian procession from Vallejo to Crockett across the new bridge. The same type of bridge walk took place when the Alfred Zampa Memorial Bridge was opened in November of 2003. (Courtesy Crockett Historical Museum.)

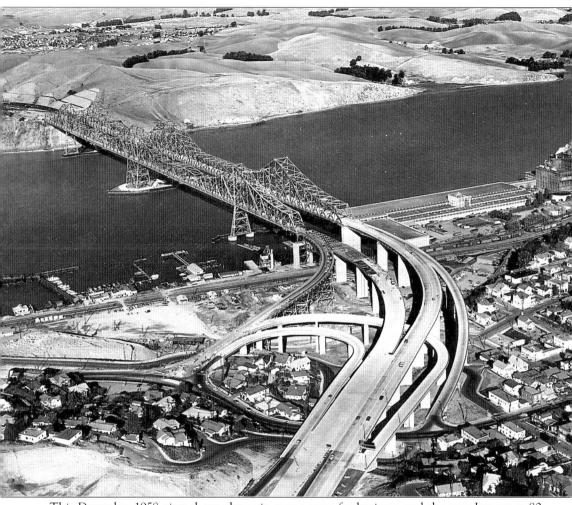

This December 1958 view shows the twin spans open for business and the new Interstate 80 almost ready for traffic. (Courtesy Crockett Historical Museum.)

Working on the second Carquinez Bridge was special to me. Like the first bridge, it was a hometown project, but more important, to me at least, was it gave me the chance to work alongside my sons Gene and Dick. I always felt pretty good about that.

—Al Zampa

Nine

BRIDGING THE SUISUN BAY

Two bridges currently span the Suisun Bay between Benicia and Martinez. The Southern Pacific train bridge was opened in 1930 and put the great train ferries *Solano* and *Contra Costa* out of business. The two ferries that had plied the Carquinez Strait between Benicia and Port Costa for 50 years made their last runs the day the train bridge was put into service. Automobile ferries still made the run between Benicia and Martinez until the second bridge, the George Miller Jr. Memorial Bridge, opened for traffic in 1963.

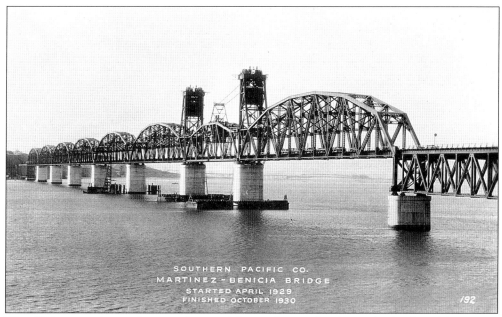

This 1931 postcard provides a good view of the newly completed train bridge from Martinez to Benicia. Construction started in April 1929, and the bridge was opened in October 1930. It was a quick construction schedule for such a large structure. This bridge is still in service.

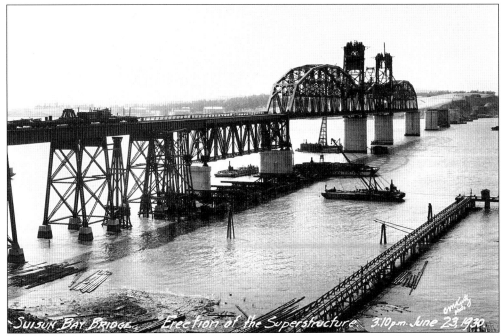

This June 1930 photograph shows the two towers and the lift span in place as the erection proceeds toward the Benicia shore.

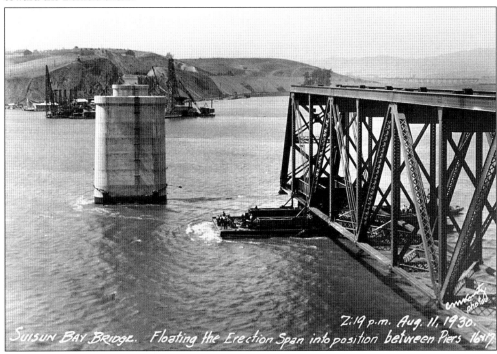

By August 1930, the bridge was half constructed. Pictured here is an erection span being floated into position between the piers. The erection span was used as a temporary falsework while the truss spans were being built. When all the trusses were constructed, the erection span was used as the final span on the Benicia shore.

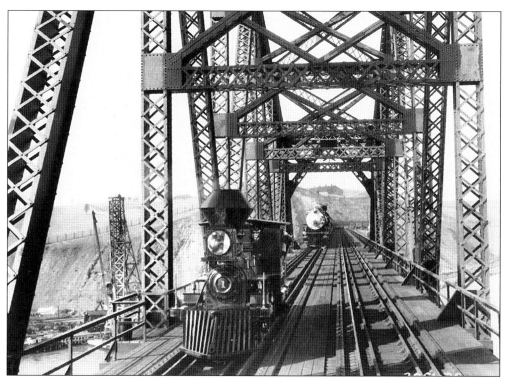

Here are the first train across the bridge, Engine No. 1, and the first modern train, following close behind.

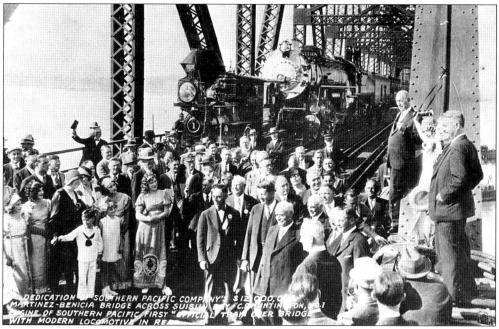

This is another view of the opening-day celebration and the dedication of Southern Pacific's $12-million lift bridge across the Suisun Bay. The first official train over the bridge was the *C. P. Huntington*, No. 1.

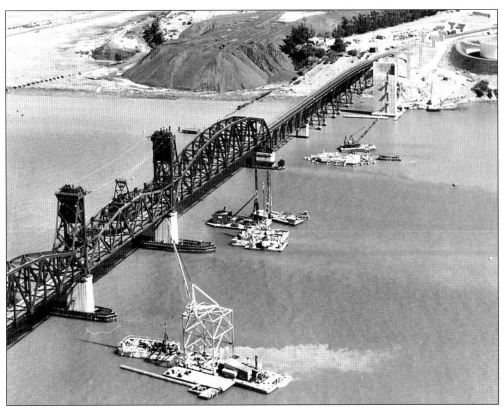

By 1961, a small armada of barge cranes, tugboats, and barges were on site to begin construction of the highway bridge between Martinez and Benicia.

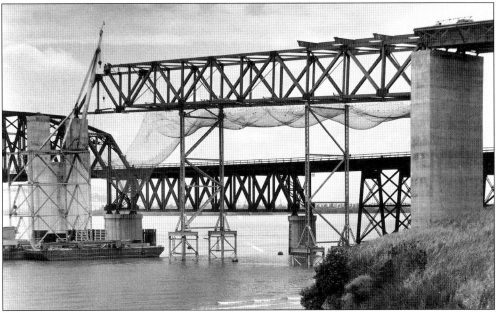

By May 1961, the deck trusses were reaching out from the Martinez shore. Note the safety nets beneath the steel.

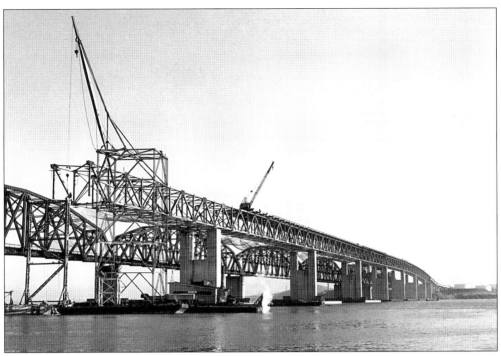

This easterly view from January 1962 shows that the deck trusses extended a half-mile into the bay.

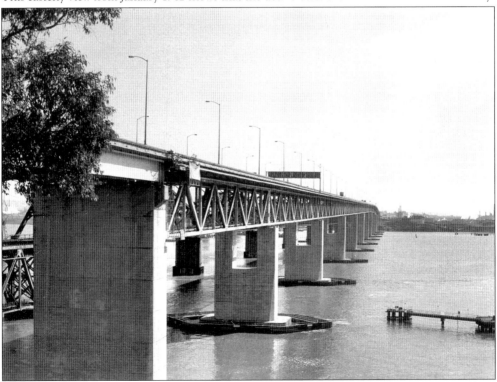

This December 2004 photograph shows the gentle arch of the mile-long deck-truss bridge. (Photograph by John V. Robinson.)

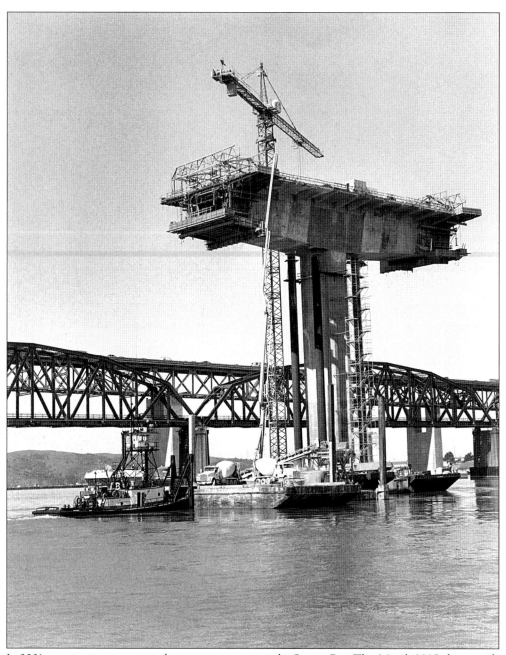

In 2001, construction was started on a new span across the Suisun Bay. This March 2005 photograph shows one of the pier tables as it grows out to the east and west using a traveler-form system. Visible in the frame are concrete trucks on barges and the boom of a pumper-truck that propels the concrete up to the forms. (Photograph by John V. Robinson.)

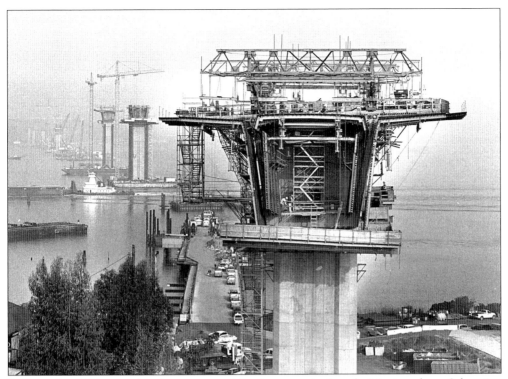

By December 2004, a traveling form structure is in place atop pier 5 on the Martinez shore. Other piers in various stages of construction are visible in the distance. (Photograph by John V. Robinson.)

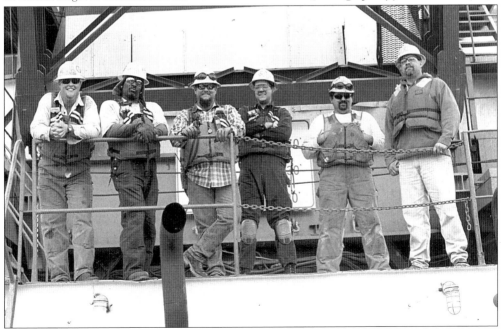

This April 2004 photograph shows the crew on barge cranes at pier 13. Pictured, from left to right, are Ben Ahlson, Doug Russell, Matt Stephens, John "McKay" Partridge, Pat Escalante, and Rob Edwards. (Photograph by John V. Robinson.)

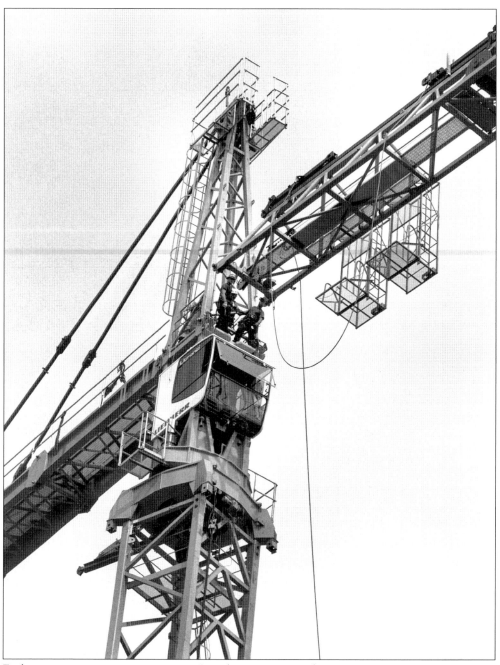

Each pier requires its own tower care. Seen here are ironworkers preparing to connect a section of the boom to the tower. (Photograph by John V. Robinson.)

Ironworkers raise the machine deck into place on the crane. The machine deck holds the counterweights, the drums and wire, and the other mechanical elements that allow the tower crane to do its work. (Photograph by John V. Robinson.)

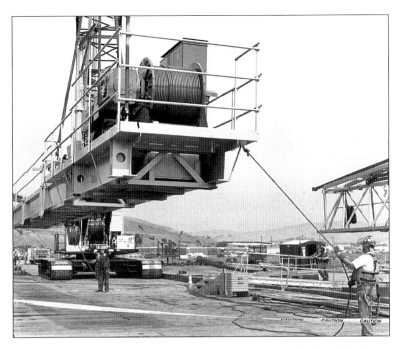

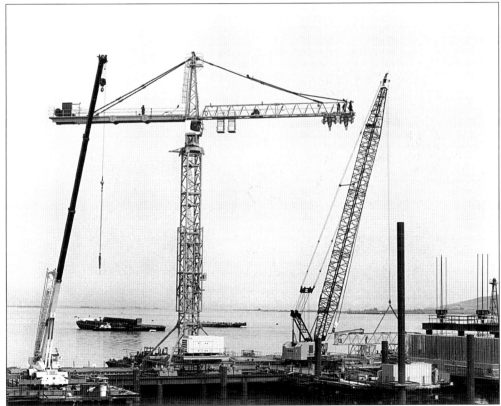

With the machine deck and first boom section in place, the bridge crew prepares to raise the last boom section into place. (Photograph by John V. Robinson.)

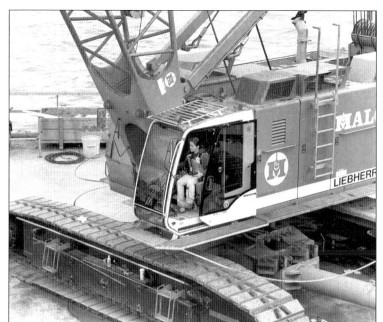

All of the materials on the bridge have to be brought to the work area by barge. Here Catherine Lytle sits at the controls of a massive Liebherr crawler crane on its own barge at pier 13. (Photograph by John V. Robinson.)

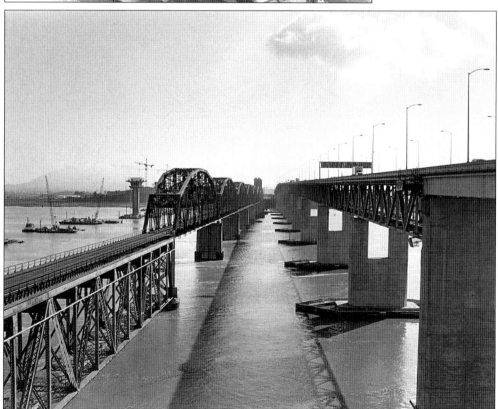

This February 2005 view, looking east from the Benicia shoreline, shows the two existing bridges and the new bridge under construction. The newest bridge across the Suisun Bay is scheduled to open in 2007. (Photograph by John V. Robinson.)

Ten

THE ALFRED ZAMPA MEMORIAL BRIDGE

Ground was broken for the third span across the strait in March 2000. The Alfred Zampa Memorial Bridge is the first suspension span built in America in over 30 years. One of the innovative construction techniques employed for the new bridge was the use of an orthotropic box-girder design.

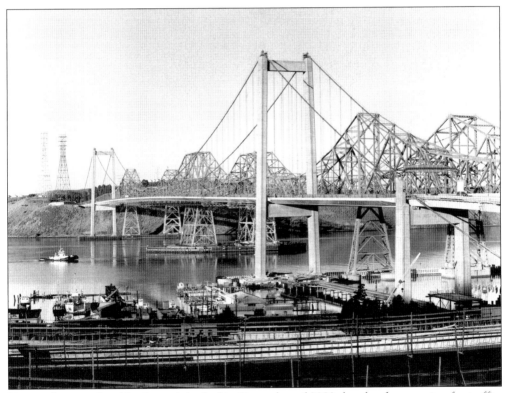

Here is the completed bridge as it looked in December of 2003 shortly after opening for traffic. The overall length of the bridge is 3,500 feet, and the main span between the towers is 2,400 feet. The road deck is about 150 feet above the water. (Photograph by John V. Robinson.)

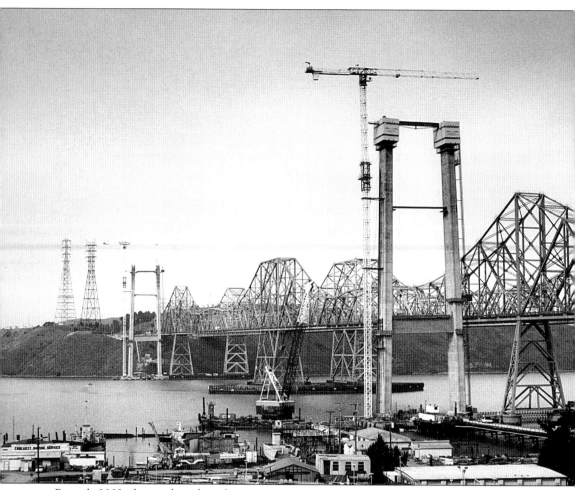

By early 2002, the north and south towers were nearing completion. Each of the 420-foot towers consists of two reinforced-concrete legs, joined by two cross struts—one at the road deck and the other at the tower top; the tower legs are hollow. The east shaft has a stairway that goes from the pier to the top, while the west shaft has a small elevator that goes the same distance. The connecting struts have passageways between the tower legs. (Photograph by John V. Robinson.)

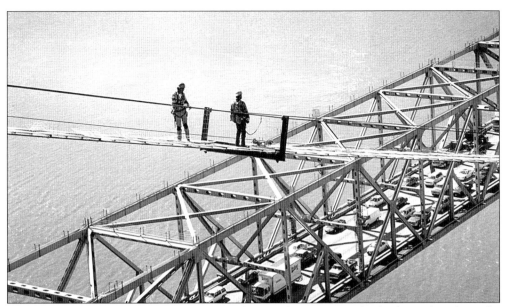

This July 2002 photograph shows two ironworkers on the main-span footbridge. Below them, the traffic congestion on the 1958 span is visible. (Photograph by John V. Robinson.)

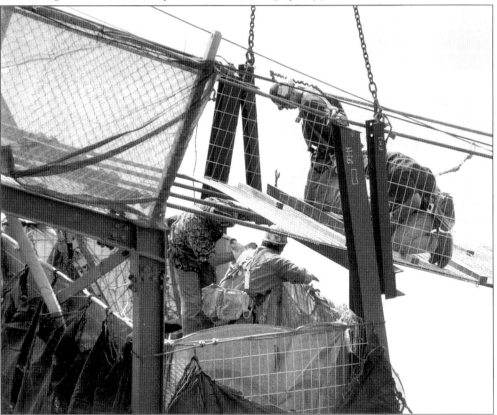

A workbasket, suspended below the floor strands, gave the ironworkers added safety and easier access as they assembled the footbridge in July 2002. (Photograph by John V. Robinson.)

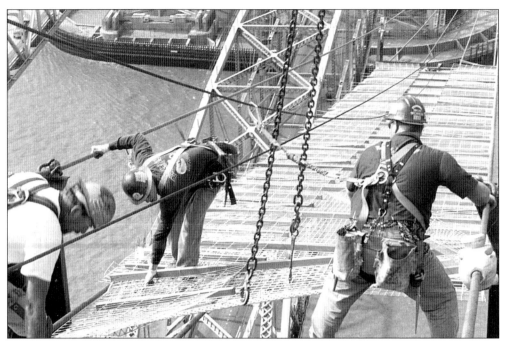

In early July 2002, ironworkers began constructing the footbridge between the two towers. It was built of wood-backed wire panels that were assembled at the tower tops into long mesh-trains that were pulled to the center of the bridge by a winch line. (Photograph by John V. Robinson)

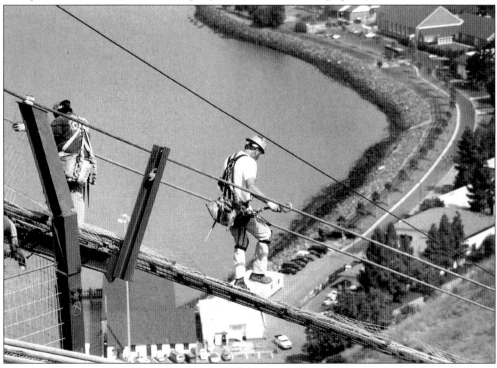

Ironworkers are seen here constructing the footbridge on the Vallejo side-span. (Photograph by John V. Robinson.)

This July 2002 image shows one set of saddle caps coming by barge to the base of the north tower. Because of their great weight, the saddle caps were cast in three pieces and assembled on the tower tops. (Photograph by John V. Robinson.)

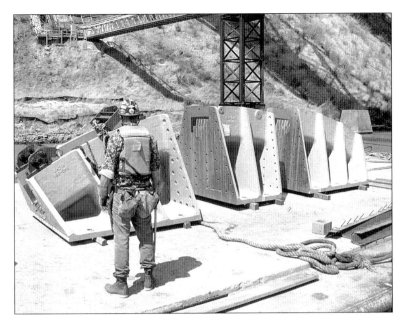

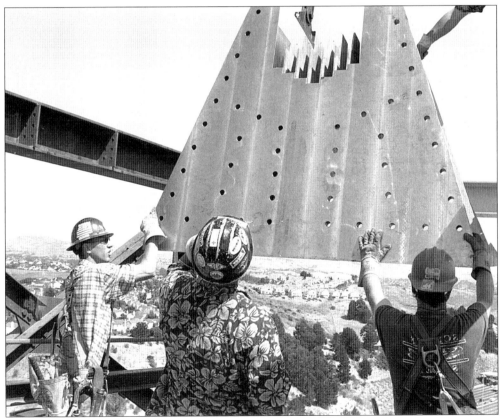

By late July 2002, the saddle caps were being placed atop the north tower of the bridge. (Photograph by John V. Robinson.)

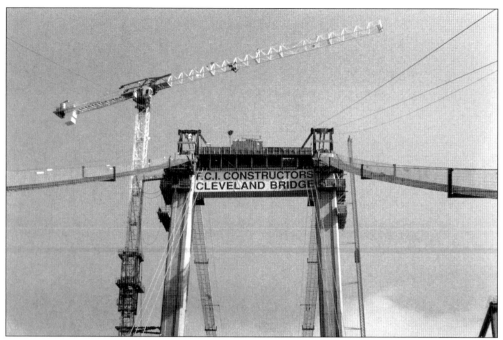

This view from August 2002 shows the top of the south tower just before the start of cable spinning. The shot was taken midway up the side-span from the cross-bridge between the two footbridges. (Photograph by John V. Robinson.)

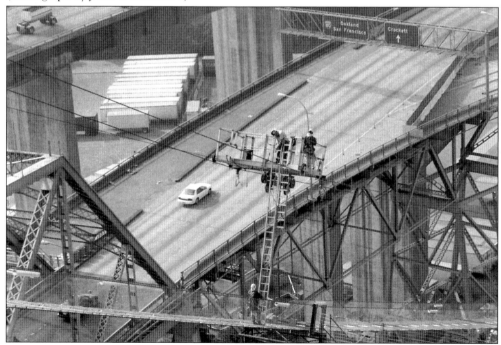

To prepare for the cable-spinning operation, a series of tram beams had to be stationed along the bridge to support the spinning wheels on the journey across the bridge. Ironworkers are here installing one of the many tram beams near the Crockett side-span. (Photograph by John V. Robinson.)

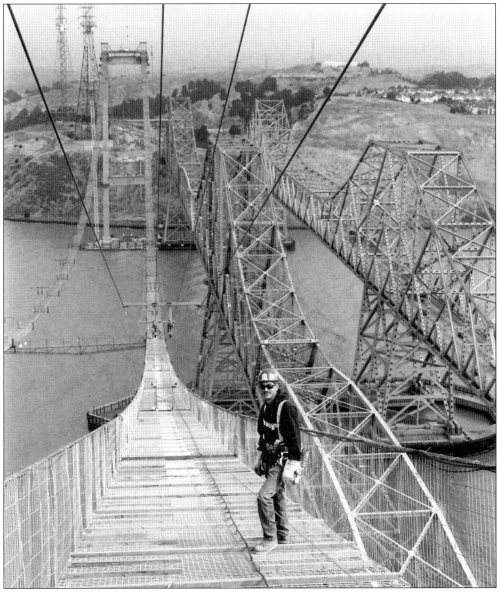

By late August 2002, the bridge was ready to begin the cable-spinning operation. Ironworker Nick Green is pictured here on the footbridge near the south tower of the bridge. (Photograph by John V. Robinson.)

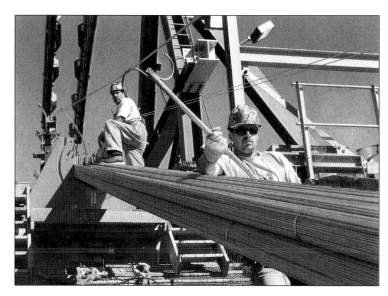

As the spinning wheel passed over the saddle cap, the wires had to be guided into their proper place on the main cable. An ironworker is seen here using a shepherd's hook to keep the wires in place. (Photograph by John V. Robinson.)

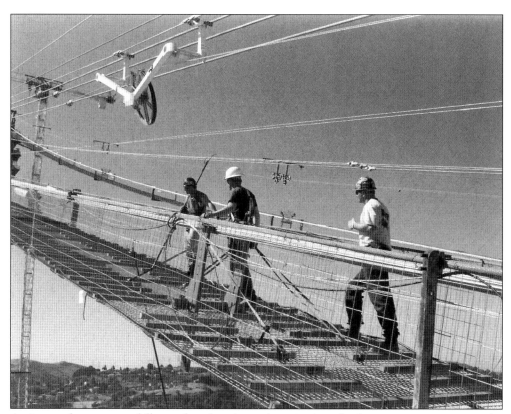

An ironworker crew carefully watches the wire as the spinning wheel starts its journey across the strait. (Photograph by John V. Robinson.)

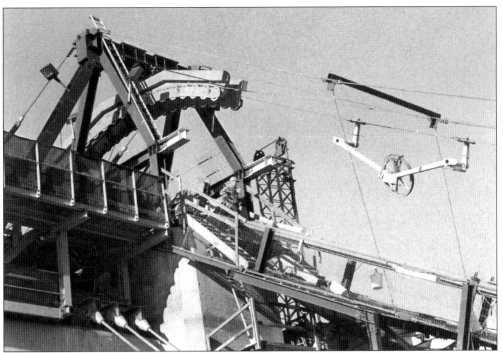

This September 2002 photograph shows the spinning wheel passing over the south tower on its journey back to the Vallejo anchorage. (Photograph by John V. Robinson.)

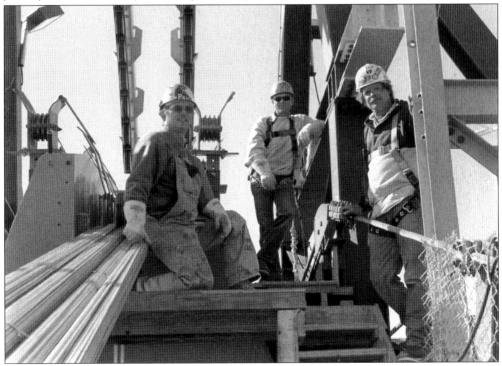

This is the spinning crew on the south tower saddle cap. Pictured, from left to right, are Paul Zorn, Norris Carter, and Curtis Staats. (Photograph by John V. Robinson.)

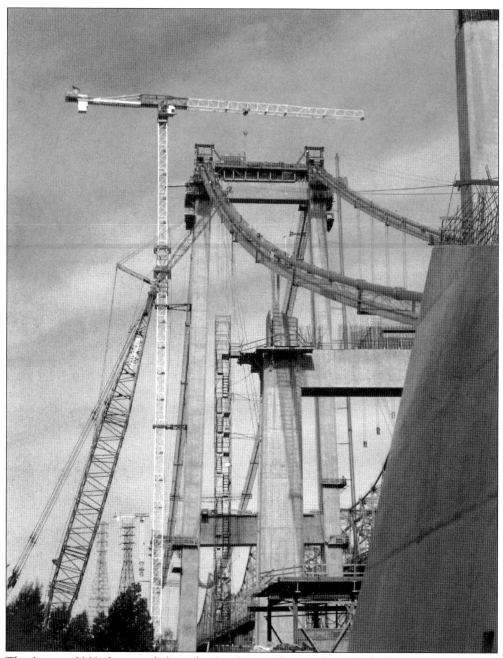

This January 2003 photograph from the Crockett anchorage shows the bridge as it appeared just before the deck sections were to arrive from Japan. (Photograph by John V. Robinson.)

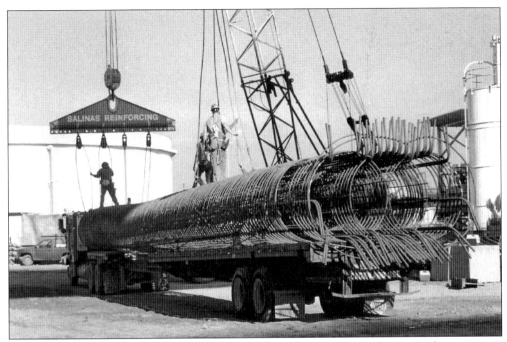

In this image, ironworkers prepare one of the 90-foot rebar columns to be put in place near the Crockett shore. Two cranes were needed for this delicate operation—one to lift the column and one to hold the base clear of the ground so it wouldn't drag and possibly fall apart. (Photograph by John V. Robinson.)

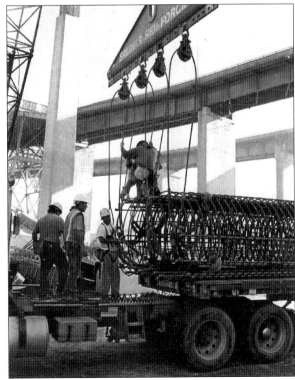

This detail view shows the rigging tackle and the spreader beam used to lift one of the massive columns into place. (Photograph by John V. Robinson.)

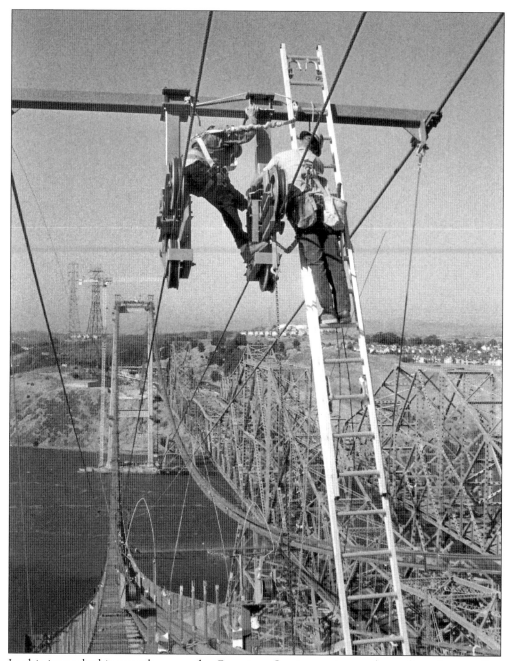

In this image looking north across the Carquinez Strait, two ironworkers adjust the tramline used in the cable-spinning operation. Modern construction workers wear full-body harnesses to protect them from a fall. The two men in this photograph are safely tied off to the tram beam. (Photograph by John V. Robinson.)

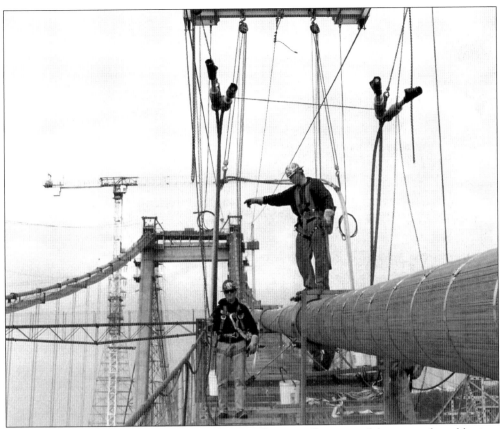

This December 2002 view shows a crew of ironworkers trundling one of the suspender cables into place on the main span. (Photograph by John V. Robinson.)

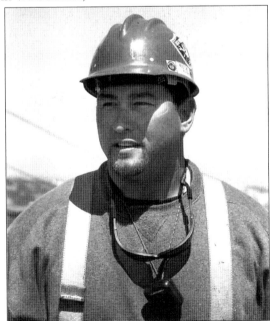

Ironworker Randy Chin is shown here on the south tower in April 2003. (Photograph by John V. Robinson)

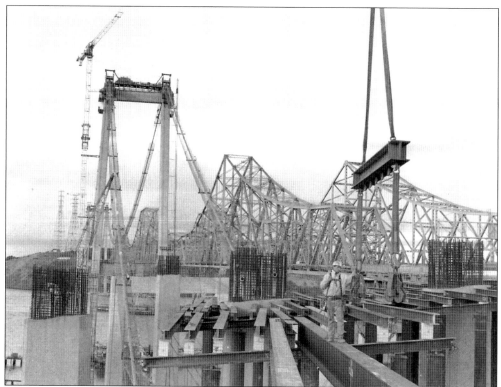

While the suspension span was under construction, a long elevated approach was being constructed under a separate contract awarded to C. C. Myers. In this photograph from November 2002, a pile driver is seen building the steel falsework into place for the new approach. (Photograph by John V. Robinson.)

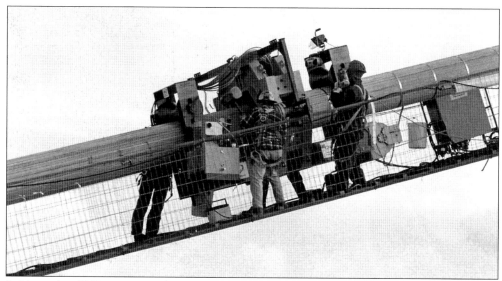

In November 2002, crews were busy compacting the main cable. The compacting machines had six 200-ton hydraulic jacks aligned in a circle to compress the main cable from a loose hexagonal shape down to a tight circle, roughly 22 inches in diameter. (Photograph by John V. Robinson.)

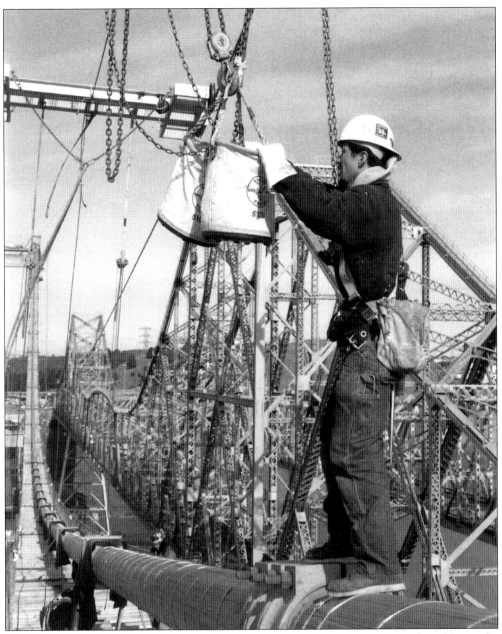

By January of 2003, bridge crews were installing the cable bands and their suspender cables, as the bridge was made ready to receive the deck sections that were en route from Japan. (Photograph by John V. Robinson.)

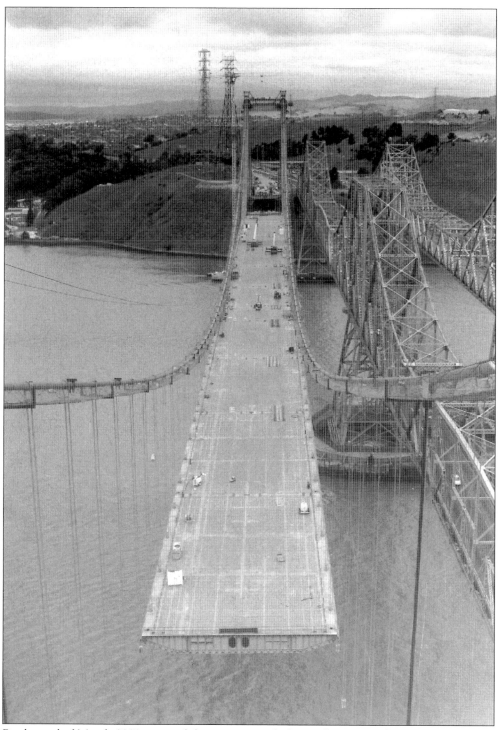

By the end of March 2003, most of the main-span deck panels were in place. The bridge was finally starting to take on a more permanent look. (Photograph by John V. Robinson.)

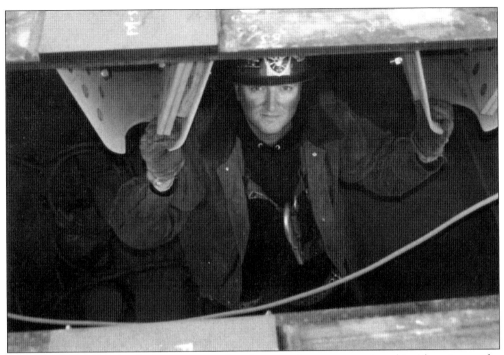

As the gap between the deck panels was closed, ironworkers were stationed inside to insert the hundreds of bolts needed to secure the connections. It was loud work in a dark and confined space—not a good place to be claustrophobic. (Photograph by John V. Robinson.)

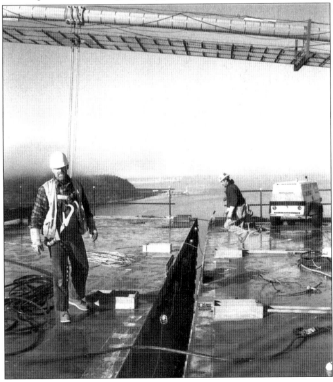

This shot from early March 2003 shows one of the 600-ton deck panels in place. A set of hydraulic jacks was employed to close the gap. (Photograph by John V. Robinson.)

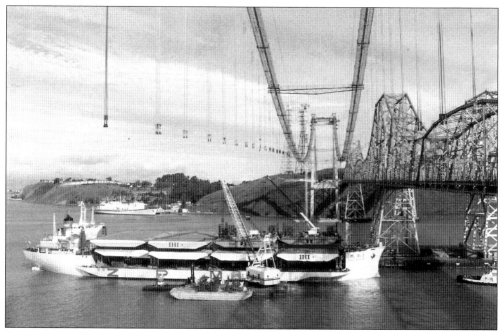

Deck-lifting operations were hampered by several days of heavy fog in the strait. On Sunday, February 2, the weather finally broke and the transport *Zhenhua 5* was securely moored beneath the bridge, ready to send the first deck panel up to the waiting bridge crew. (Photograph by John V. Robinson.)

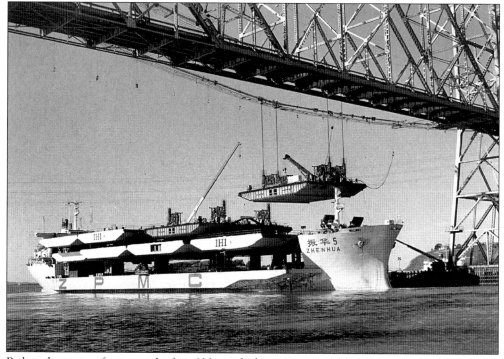

By late that same afternoon, the first 600-ton deck section was safely on its way up to ironworkers waiting on the footbridge above the ship. (Photograph by John V. Robinson.)

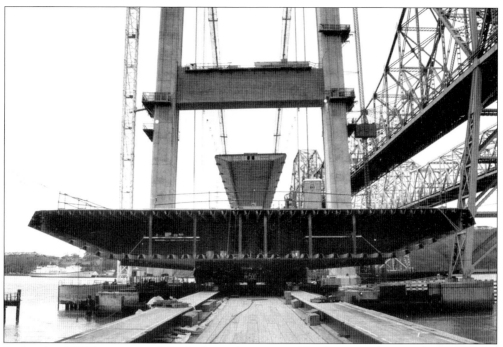

In this April 2003 view, one of the deck panels, supported by the carrier beams, slowly makes its way down the trestle toward the Crockett shoreline. Some of these sections weighed as much as 600 tons. (Photograph by John V. Robinson.)

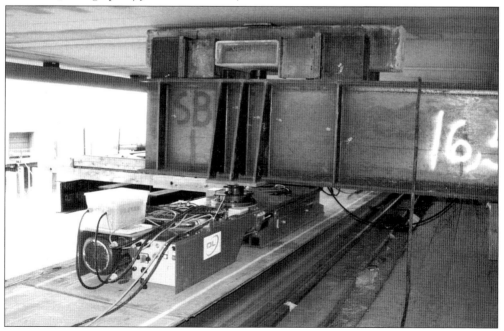

A detail of one of the hydraulic walkers is seen in this image. The south shore deck panels were set on carrier beams supported by four hydraulic walkers (called "johnny walkers" by the bridge workers) that slowly lifted and transferred the weight of the panels down the trestle. (Photograph by John V. Robinson.)

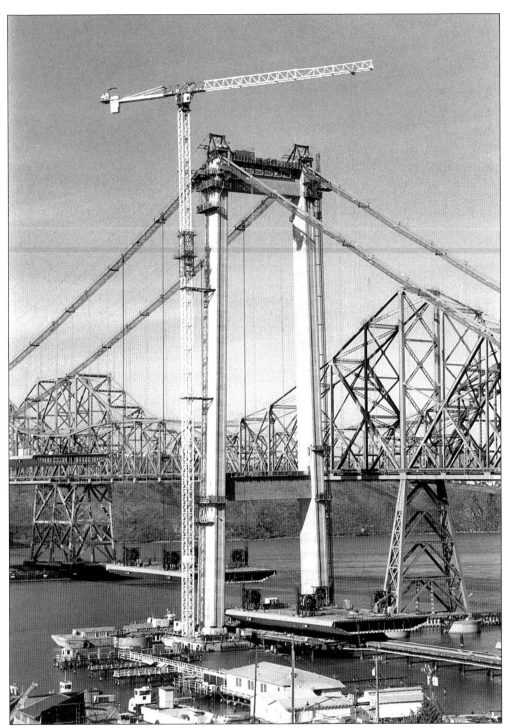

After the deck panels were lifted off the deck of the ship, they were pulled laterally between the legs of the south tower and landed on the trestle. Once safely on the trestle, the panels were skidded into position with hydraulic walkers and lifted into place. (Photograph by John V. Robinson.)

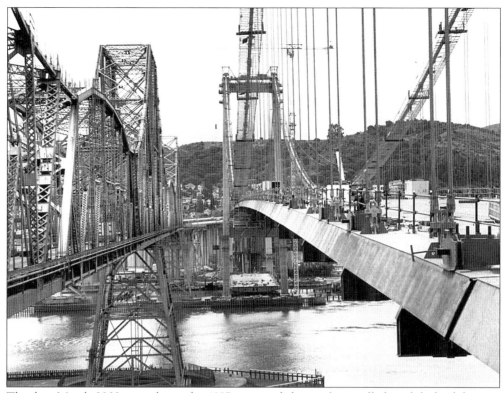

This late March 2003 view shows the 1927 span and the newly installed road deck of the new bridge. In the distance, two deck panels can be seen on the trestle beneath the south tower. (Photograph by John V. Robinson.)

In early April 2003, one of the final deck panels is lifted into position and pulled into place by lateral jacks. Here, ironworker Brian Colombo installs jack strand for one of the lateral pulls. (Photograph by John V. Robinson.)

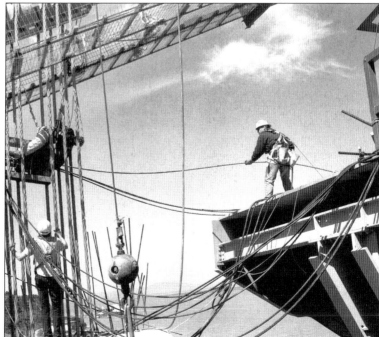

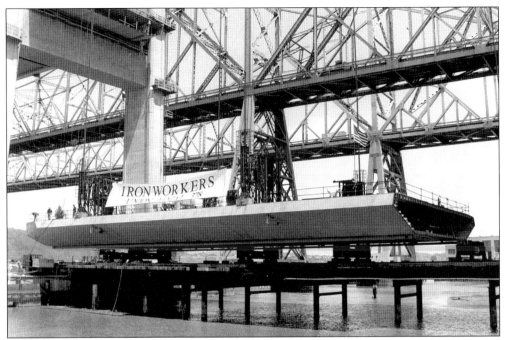

A long-standing tradition in the construction industry is called "topping out." The final deck panel is seen here festooned with a banner, an evergreen tree (visible in the far left corner), and an American flag (right corner) being hoisted into place on the bridge. (Photograph by John V. Robinson.)

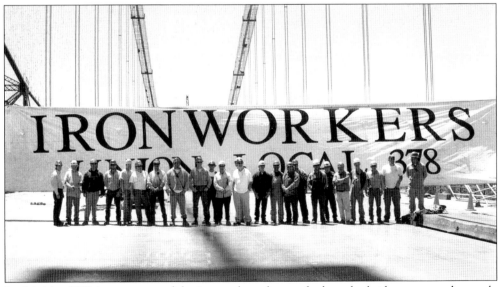

In this May 2003 image, some of the ironworkers that worked on the bridge pose on the newly completed road deck. Pictured, from left to right, are Don Zampa, Ed Millican, Kenny Buntjer, Harry ?, Brad Fisher, Dick McCabe, Darrin Bessolo, Randy Chin, Ken Miller, Brice Mouser, Brian Colombo, Mark Ferguson, Bob Vine, Scott Seymour, John Pendleton, unidentified, Roger Ruiz, unidentified, Dan Quillere, Pat Meehan, Norris Carter, and two unidentified men. (Photograph by John V. Robinson.)

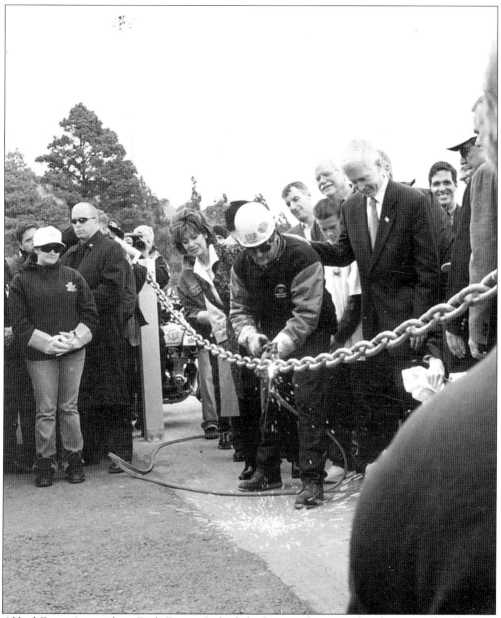

Alfred Zampa's grandson Dick Zampa Jr. had the honor of cutting the chain to officially open the Alfred Zampa Memorial Bridge. (Photograph by John V. Robinson.)

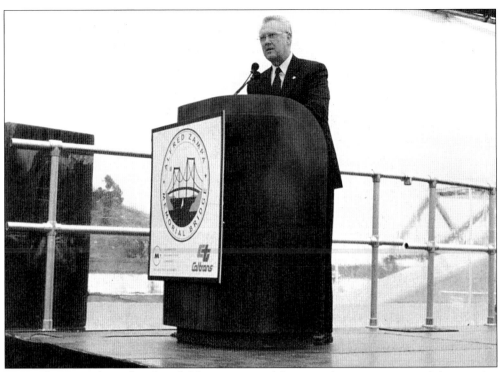

Ironworker general president Joseph Hunt was one of the many dignitaries to attend the opening celebration for the new bridge. (Photograph by John V. Robinson.)

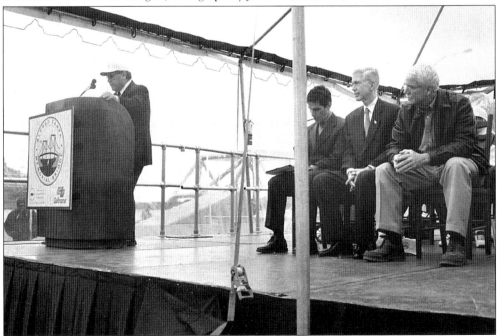

Among the other speakers at the November 2003 opening of the Alfred Zampa Memorial Bridge were, from left to right, Dick Zampa, speaking; Caltrans director Jeff Morales; Gov. Gray Davis; and Congressman George Miller. (Photograph by John V. Robinson.)

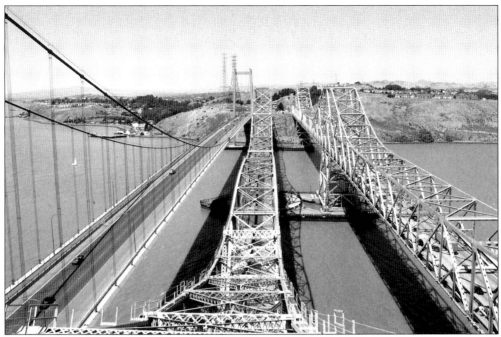

This September 2004 view was photographed from the top of the south anchor arm of the 1927 bridge. The old bridge is slated for demolition in 2006. (Photograph by John V. Robinson.)

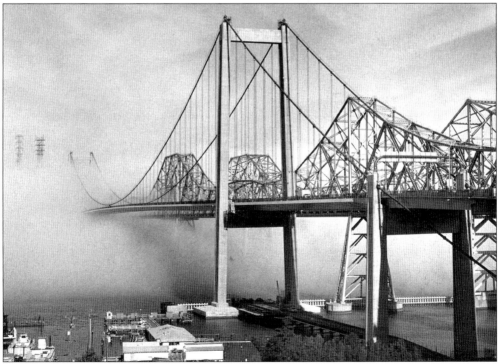

This beautiful January 2005 view of the three bridges shrouded in fog shows why the new bridge's pedestrian walkway is a popular destination for cyclists, joggers, and walkers. (Photograph by John V. Robinson.)

BIBLIOGRAPHY

Adams, Charles F. *Heroes of the Golden Gate*. Palo Alto: Pacific Books, 1987.

Berson, Misha. "Fingerprints on Steel." *San Francisco Examiner*. Image. May 10, 1987.

Blakely, Scott. "He Built Them All, Large and Small. *San Francisco Chronicle*, November 4, 1986.

California Toll Bridges and Bay Area Tunnels & Tubes. California Department of Transportation. September 1978.

Cassady, Stephen. *Spanning the Gate*. Mill Valley, CA. Squarebooks, 1987.

Dedication Souvenir. Carquinez Bridge Celebration. May 21, 1927.

Dillon, Richard, Thomas Moulin, and Don Denevi. *High Steel: Building the Bridges Across the San Francisco Bay*. Berkeley: Celestial Arts, 1979.

Halfway to Hell 1987. Videocassette. San Francisco: Labor Video Project.

Jennings, James B. et al. *The Richmond San Rafael Bridge: A Photographic Story*. Richmond, CA: 1955.

Lochner, Tom. "Building a Bridge in the 21st Century." *West County Times*. March 4, 2000.

_____. "Famed Bridge Builder Al Zampa Dies." *West County Times*. April 25, 2000.

Maynard, Isabelle. Interviews with the author. Emeryville, CA: 2001–2003.

Mensch, E. Cromwell. *The Golden Gate Bridge. A Technical Description in Ordinary Language*. San Francisco: privately printed, 1935.

"Net Saves First Worker to Fall Off Gate Bridge." *San Francisco Chronicle*. October 17, 1936.

"Net Grounded; Bridge Worker Falls; May Die." *San Francisco Chronicle*. October 20, 1936.

Ney, Bart. "The Carquinez Connection." *Crockett Signal*. 2002–2003.

_____. *Spanning the Carquinez Strait: The Alfred Zampa Memorial Bridge*. Sacramento: California Department of Transportation, 2003.

Pereira, Joseph. "Bridge Builder Lived to Tell the Tale." *West County Times*. September 22, 1986.

Plowden, David. *Bridges: The Spans of North America*. New York: W. W. Norton, 1974.

Raddue, Gordon. "How He Joined the 'Half Way to Hell Club." *Contra Costa Independent*. January 6, 1983.

Seaver, Lynda. "Bay Bridge was Builders' Baby, Despite the Danger." *Oakland Tribune*. October 26, 1986.

Spencer, Richard. "Carquinez Bridge is Granddaddy of Them All." *Oakland Tribune*. October 16, 1986.

Trimble, Paul C. and John C. Alioto Jr. *The Bay Bridge*. San Francisco: Arcadia Publishing, 2005.

Van Der Zee, John. *The Gate*. New York: Simon and Schuster, 1986.

Winn, Bernard C. *California Drawbridges (1853–1995)*. San Francisco: Incline Press, 1995.

Wolman, Baron and Tom Horton. *Superspan: the Golden Gate Bridge*. San Francisco: Chronicle Books, 1983.